"I would recommend any book Collin Ha[...]
of the most thoughtful and devout men [...]
about what full-orbed and united ministry looks like [...] p[...]
culture, I *enthusiastically* recommend it. The church has a big job in this
era, and Hansen's book helps us face into it with courage, compassion,
and conviction."

Mark Galli, Editor, *Christianity Today*

"Collin Hansen is one of the best younger writers and thinkers in the
Lord's church today. Here he calls on followers of Jesus to manifest three
marks, each of which is essential for full-orbed discipleship: holy bold-
ness, loving kindness, and a gospel witness that crosses all bounds."

Timothy George, Founding Dean, Beeson Divinity School;
General Editor, *Reformation Commentary on Scripture*

"Courage to speak the truth, compassion to care for the broken and
the oppressed, commissioned to evangelize and plant churches—but
how often do all three of these commitments meld together, surfacing
as unified Christian maturity in our churches? The simple thesis of this
book is that eager submission to the Lord Jesus requires such a unified
vision. To opt for only one of these commitments while dismissing those
who opt for others is to turn aside from Scripture while flirting with
sterility and ugliness."

D. A. Carson, Research Professor of New Testament,
Trinity Evangelical Divinity School

"This book is Collin at his best. With humility and wit, he examines
our moment in history and asks, What is wrong with the church? Collin's answer: I am. From that vantage point we begin to understand
the beautiful thing God is doing in our generation, encompassing the
various gifts he has placed in different Christian traditions. Collin is
confident enough in his convictions to write with clarity and authority,
yet humble enough to learn from others. This book not only provides
insight; it models how to learn from others."

J. D. Greear, Lead Pastor, The Summit Church, Durham, North
Carolina; author, *Jesus, Continued . . . Why the Spirit Inside You
Is Better than Jesus Beside You*

"Collin Hansen provides a valuable framework to the evangelical community to assess our witness and examine our weaknesses in light of Christ's strengths. This book provides timely, helpful, winsome, and wise counsel for believers seeking to encourage others and effectively expand their witness to a watching world."

Ed Stetzer, President, LifeWay Research; author,
Subversive Kingdom; www.edstetzer.com

"Collin Hansen is a thoughtful and wise leader. This book will help equip all of us to ask what we're not seeing in the mission field around us and in our own lives. You will find this book both convicting and rejuvenating at the same time."

Russell D. Moore, President, The Ethics & Religious Liberty
Commission; author, *Tempted and Tried*

"This is a little book that goes to war against all of the right enemies: self-righteousness, pomposity, and anger misplaced. Let's face it. We've heard enough of our 'heroes' thunder from the mountaintops. We've planted accusatory fingers into the chests of our fellow believers. We've lamented a culture in decline. The truth be told, we're sick of our own Twitter and Facebook feeds. In response to all of these, Collin Hansen knows the source of the problem. It's you. It's me. And in the spirit of Carl F. H. Henry's 'sober optimism,' he points us back to the compassion of Christ for a remedy."

Gregory Alan Thornbury, President, The King's College; author,
Recovering Classic Evangelicalism

"Collin Hansen offers the multifaceted evangelical church an incisive, sympathetic approach to self-diagnosis. Here is a hopeful vision in which our differences are not ultimately obstacles but opportunities for greater unity in courage, compassion, and commissioning. My hope is that this brief book will win a broad hearing."

Stephen T. Um, Senior Minister, Citylife Presbyterian Church,
Boston, Massachusetts; co-author, *Why Cities Matter*

BLIND SPOTS

Becoming a Courageous, Compassionate,
and Commissioned Church

COLLIN HANSEN

Foreword by
TIM KELLER

WHEATON, ILLINOIS

Blind Spots: Becoming a Courageous, Compassionate, and *Commissioned Church*

Copyright © 2015 by Collin Hansen

Published by Crossway
    1300 Crescent Street
    Wheaton, Illinois 60187

Published in association with the literary agency of Wolgemuth & Associates, Inc.

Cover design: Josh Dennis

First printing 2015

Printed in the United States of America

Trade paperback ISBN: 978-1-4335-4623-5
ePub ISBN: 978-1-4335-4626-6
PDF ISBN: 978-1-4335-4624-2
Mobipocket ISBN: 978-1-4335-4625-9

Library of Congress Cataloging-in-Publication Data
Hansen, Collin, 1981–
 Blind spots : becoming a courageous, compassionate, and commissioned church / Collin Hansen ; foreword by Tim Keller.
   pages cm. — (Cultural renewal)
  Includes bibliographical references and index.
  ISBN 978-1-4335-4623-5 (tp)
  1. Church—Unity. 2. Evangelicalism. 3. Christianity and culture. 4. Mission of the church. 5. Edwards, Jonathan, 1703–1758. I. Title.
BV601.5.H355   2015
280'.042—dc23   2014039166

Crossway is a publishing ministry of Good News Publishers.

VP		25	24	23	22	21	20	19	18	17	16	15
15	14	13	12	11	10	9	8	7	6	5	4	3	2	1

Contents

Foreword

Tim Keller

Jonathan Edwards was keenly interested in the philosophy and thought of his day, and at the same time he was fully committed to the absolute authority of the Scriptures. As a result he was, as Richard Lints put it, "arguably the most creative and the most orthodox theologian [at once] that America has ever produced."[1] Edwards was also as deeply committed to sound, systematic biblical doctrine as he was fascinated by the workings of the heart and how the emotions and senses relate to our reason. This meant, "He stands with Augustine and Luther in the depth of his analysis of religious experience, [and] he stands with Aquinas and Calvin in the breadth of his intellectual grasp of the gospel."[2]

This breadth of interest is, however, extraordinarily hard to maintain. Historian Mark A. Noll demonstrates this in his essay "Jonathan Edwards and Nineteenth-Century Theology," in which he traces out Edwards's legacy in the American church over the hundred years or so after his death.[3]

Old Princeton, including Charles Hodge and B. B. Warfield, were the most true to Edwards's orthodox Reformed theology. However, not only were they "far from independent or original thinkers"; they were increasingly inattentive to matters of revival and spiritual experience.[4] Edwards's New England disciples such as Samuel Hopkins, Jonathan Edwards Jr., and later Nathaniel Taylor were social activists, abolitionists, and creative theological thinkers, but they left behind much of Edwards's biblically faithful doctrine. So did Charles Finney, an enthusiastic reader of Edwards on revivals who strongly rejected his Reformed theology.[5]

Noll's essay demonstrates that there were some who maintained Edwards's doctrinal orthodoxy, some who adopted his creative cultural engagement, and some who kept his enthusiasm for revivals and mission.[6] Ironically, each of these parties claiming Edwards as inspiration was hostile and critical toward the others during much of the early nineteenth century. Some theologians and ministers kept these various strands—doctrine, cultural engagement, and revival—interwoven and integrated, but that was not true of most.[7]

You must not think by this foreword that Collin Hansen's book is about church history or the historic schools of American Reformed theology. It is not at all. Rather, it is an extended essay on how Christians in Western societies today are responding and how they need to respond to a culture quickly growing post-Christian. Christians have not come to consensus on how to respond to this new world. Collin sees us fragmenting into at least three distinct responses, each with its own peculiar blind spots, and each one highly critical of the other two.

The three parties of Edwards's followers correspond roughly to the groups that Collin discerns on the scene today. This is evidence that these fissures within our ranks have been with us for a long time and that each party has latched onto some true aspect of what it means to live the Christian life. The "courage" group stands valiantly for the truth; the "compassion" people stress service, listening, and engagement; while the "commissioned" folks are all about building up the church and reaching the lost. Once things are broken down like that, it becomes clear that these should be strands in a single cord. Each group goes bad to the degree it distances itself from the others.

I am, of course, here making this much simpler than it is. Within the pages that follow, Collin Hansen judiciously weighs and discusses the complexities of where we are and what must be done.

Acknowledgments

I'm honored that so many trusted friends and colleagues would read this book and offer detailed, constructive feedback. Turns out you need this critical insight even more when you dare to write a book about blind spots in the church, because these friends help you see your own.

My editor Justin Taylor has always modeled Christlike friendship and genuine humility in an industry where you can't take it for granted.

Supremely gifted writers Trevin Wax and Kevin DeYoung saved me from some of my most egregious oversights. I'm privileged to read and share their writing on a nearly daily basis through The Gospel Coalition (TGC).

Andrew Wolgemuth somehow found time to shape the organization and tone of this book between our discussions about the Kansas City Royals.

Betsy Childs has generously shared her friendship and professional expertise as we work together at Beeson Divinity School.

My fellow TGC editors inspired this work before I knew I

wanted to write it. John Starke and Matt Smethurst, in particular, sharpened my thinking through countless conversations about the kind of churches we hope TGC can support. All of us look up to D. A. Carson and Tim Keller, who were living out the hope of a revived and reformed church before any of us was born.

I doubt I would have captured the positive vision for this book apart from the example of the pastors and my fellow members at Redeemer Community Church in Birmingham, Alabama. I write because I've seen what's possible when a local church dares to strive in the power of the Spirit toward obeying everything Jesus commanded.

As always my toughest and kindest editor was the matchless Lauren Hansen. During the two and a half years that this book was in the works, our lives reached excruciating lows and climbed to unexpected heights. We dedicate this book to our son, Paul Carter Hansen, in the hope that he might learn to love and trust the Lord Jesus Christ in a courageous, compassionate, and commissioned church.

Introduction

I wrote this book because my arguments stopped working.

I pointed to Bible verses. I appealed to reason. I turned to church history. Nothing changed with my opponents.

Courage, I concluded by their lack of desired response, must be sorely lacking among Christians today. And that may well be true, at least when compared to our courageous hero Jesus Christ, who conquered sin by his selfless sacrifice on the cross and triumphant victory in the resurrection.

Maybe you're like me and inclined to think that courage is the chief need of the church today. We like to think of ourselves as brave and therefore willing to stand by God's Word and stand up to enemies of the gospel. So when we think of contentious issues such as homosexuality, we tend to see two camps: those who have courage and side with God, and everyone else, who sides with the world against God.

So how do we proceed when our arguments don't work? How do we persuade friends, family, and neighbors who just can't agree? You can yell louder. You can type faster and in ALL CAPS. You can threaten. You can accuse. You can make the argument personal. But you and I both know these approaches usually don't work. We've tried them. And we have the scars to show for our well-intentioned folly.

I don't know the exact details of your story. So let me tell you a little about mine to see if you can relate. I grew up in a stable family in a close-knit community, as someone bred to appreciate history and respect authority. I learned about God in Sunday school classes and children's sermons, but I was not raised in a home that talked about Jesus or in a church that preached the gospel. So imagine the shock of my friends and family when at age fifteen I was born again to new life with Jesus. They were more perplexed than angry. Even so, I learned at an early age that I must choose either to deny my Savior or defy my loved ones' expectations. In short I learned that to follow Jesus demands courage. Not coincidentally I bonded in college with the woman who would become my wife, as she shared a similar experience of turning to Christ at the end of high school. And in this private university, where our faith felt regularly under attack by classmates and professors, we typically befriended other Christians who followed Jesus with passion and courage.

I thank God that when he called me, he showed me the cost of discipleship. But many years passed before I truly understood that my experience is not normative for every Christian. I had a hard time relating to Christians who grew up in churches with hypocritical leaders who shackled them with unbiblical traditions. If these believers stayed in the church, they tended to practice a softer kind of Christianity, more enamored with the compassionate Jesus who pardoned the woman caught in adultery (John 8:1–11) than the righteous Jesus who overturned tables in the temple (John 2:13–22). And don't get me started on the Christians I met in churches who never seemed to move on from the basics about Jesus. They were so busy hyping Jesus with high-energy sermons and upbeat music and message-driven T-shirts that they didn't make any time to talk with me about theology, church history, or the challenges of following Jesus in our consumeristic culture.

With my highly attuned gift for discerning others' motives, it didn't take long for me to see what's wrong with everyone else. Then I blamed them for not seeing the wisdom in my arguments. It took longer to realize that my experience does not exhaust the example of Jesus. And when I finally compared my life to Jesus, as he's revealed across four multifaceted Gospels and the rest of the New Testament, I began to see my own sin, my blind spots. Because I had understood my experience as normative for everyone, I couldn't see how God blessed other Christians with different stories and strengths. Yes, they needed to develop discernment, knowledge, and courage. But God wanted me to see how we would be stronger together in the body of Christ as we worked according to our unique gifts.

I may not share or even understand your experiences. Maybe you're more successful than I am when arguing with people who are different from you. In any event, I know that unless we can both step outside ourselves to hear our arguments from another vantage point, we won't enjoy church unity and an effective gospel witness in the world.

You and I have been conditioned by our various cultures and experiences to hear certain aspects of the gospel more clearly than others. When I first responded to the gospel, I didn't hear the good news about Jesus in its fullness. In fact, no one really told me anything about repenting of sin. But as an insecure high school sophomore, I wanted to fit in with older teenagers I admired. I only knew they radiated joy I had never seen before. They saw beauty in God that had never been apparent to me in years of churchgoing. And I wanted what they had—whatever the cost.

Wherever you come from, God doesn't leave you where he found you. This process of growing in grace and holiness can be painful. I know that in my nearly two decades of following him, Jesus has been less concerned with bolstering my self-esteem and helping me fit in with friends than with putting to death my sin and any other hindrance to trusting him. Likewise, your growing love for the gospel will not remove you from your history, experience, and culture. As Jesus progressively reveals himself to you, however, his glorious light will help you see yourself a little more like he does—as God's beloved child eagerly awaiting Jesus's triumphant return.

Compared to Christ

I didn't write this book so you could find popularity with the world or make peace with one another at the expense of the revealed truth of God's Word. Controversy, disagreement, and persecution do not necessarily indicate sin on our part. They will often result from obeying Scripture and opposing false teachers (1 Tim. 1:3–11; 6:2b–10; 2 Pet. 2:1–22; Jude 3). And, actually, when we consider church unity more important than gospel truth, we end up pointing fingers and naming enemies. Consider the ecumenical movement of the twentieth century, which actually resulted in much sinful division as many churches abandoned the gospel and criticized congregations that did not follow them out of Christianity.

Nor did I write this book so I could criticize the famous Christian leaders you have in mind. Don't expect me to name names here. In what follows I am not so much thinking about the Big Name Leaders as I am about you and me. I'm aiming to help you in self-diagnosis. I wrote this book so you might learn to compare yourself more to Christ than to other Christians. When you and I compare ourselves to Christ, we get unity because we see our sin and forgive one another as God forgave us (Matt. 18:35; Eph. 4:32). When you and I compare ourselves to Christ, we reserve final judgment—your differences will primarily help me test whether I'm missing anything about the character of Jesus. When you and I compare ourselves to Christ, we're more impressed with the grace he lavished on us than with our own contributions to the kingdom.

"Jesus Christ, being himself the only God-man, who gave himself as the only ransom for sinners, is the only mediator between God and people," the Lausanne Covenant explains.

"When people receive Christ they are born again into his kingdom and must seek not only to exhibit but also to spread its righteousness in the midst of an unrighteous world."[8]

I wrote this book with the hope that you would understand the power of the gospel to expose our blind spots so that we could see our differences as opportunity. It is the will of God to put to death our sin and unite our hearts with his so that we can love our neighbors as ourselves. For example, my heart is full of thankfulness to God for the testimony delivered by a woman who began coming to our church about a year ago. She didn't know her need for Jesus until she saw community in the fellowship of the redeemed. After her first visit to our home group, she asked the friend who invited her, "That can't be what church is really like, is it?" She knew nothing but the stereotypes. She knew nothing of the grace and forgiveness.

When she recently returned to her hometown for a visit, she met with a group of friends from her former life. At first she enjoyed their company, but when the small talk ended she recoiled at their judgmental, critical attitudes. She knew she'd been no different before Jesus saved her from her sins. And she gave thanks for the abundant life she now enjoyed as a Christian in fellowship with the church. As a new creation in Christ (2 Cor. 5:17), delivered from the domain of darkness and transferred to the kingdom of Jesus (Col. 1:13), she's growing in holiness and sharing the gospel with family and coworkers.

You won't see this woman's story on the evening news.

The evangelical website I edit probably won't even feature her. But if we have the eyes of faith, we can see righteousness spreading through this unrighteous world.

Reposition and Repent

By entrusting ourselves to Jesus, we need to be willing to reposition and repent wherever necessary. You and I won't always agree on the direction Jesus aims to take us. And when we disagree, we need to hear each other in humility and test this teaching according to the Scriptures. We're not trying to defeat each other; rather, we speak truth in love so that fellow believers will "grow up in every way into him who is the head, into Christ" (Eph. 4:15). We share one Spirit—the Spirit who baptized us into the body of Christ (1 Cor. 12:13), who illumined God's Word (2 Pet. 1:21), who raised Jesus from the dead (Rom. 8:11). We may live in troubling times, but the times do not trouble this God. One day you and I will rule this world together with Christ. Take heart! Jesus has overcome the world (John 16:33), so we can overcome evil with good (Rom. 12:21).

The stakes of our cooperation are high. The world needs bold, united followers of Jesus because Christians make the best critics. You might not introduce yourself to a friend that way, but think about our global predicament. Circumstances in this chaotic world have vindicated the biblical perspective. Christians are naturally skeptical of an earthly hope or promise of revolutionary change. We trust no politician who promises to make all our dreams come true. We know wishful thinking ends in sure disappointment. We're full of faith and beholden to no one. We make the best citizens in any culture but feel at home in none of them.[9] We find common ground with various worldviews but resist any attempt to co-opt our support.

We know the debates of our age but question the failed assumptions that strangely persist. We're neither hopeless nor especially hopeful for this age. We're marked by "sober optimism," to borrow a phrase from theologian Carl F. H. Henry. As the apostle Paul observed, we're "sorrowful, yet always rejoicing" (2 Cor. 6:10). You and I can love our neighbors with the confidence that eventually righteousness will triumph, that God can ignite revival at any time. We enjoy unity because we share the same purpose: that one day every knee should bow and tongue confess that Jesus is Lord.

My arguments may have failed, but God's Word never does. We must not shrink from the times; after all, no problem we face can ever surpass what the disciples endured after Jesus's death on the cross. Imagine their confusion, their hopelessness, their feelings of rejection. Then imagine their joy mingled with doubt on the third day. Imagine how they felt when they saw their Savior again. Don't you want that freedom and confidence? The same power and the same hope belong to you and me. Jesus, the apostles, and the early church show us how to change the world even when we don't control any levers of power.

This book may sting at times. As God did with me, he may

reveal your blind spots and guide you in repentance for sin and in forgiveness for others you've wronged in word and deed. But this book is about seeing our differences as opportunity. God created us in splendid diversity of thought, experience, and personality. And when these differences cohere around the gospel of Jesus Christ, they work together to challenge, comfort, and compel a needy world with the only love that will never fail or fade.

1

Pointed Fingers and Helping Hands

It can be embarrassing to identify as a Christian. Every time you turn on your smartphone, car radio, or cable TV, someone is mocking your antiquated, harsh, prudish religion. You'd better avert your eyes from the comments sections and message boards. You don't want to scroll your mentions on Twitter. And that's just the Christians talking about each other. Sure, we've lost some credibility with the culture. But how did we also lose trust in one another inside the church?

You're not sure whom to believe in this hazardous climate of perpetual outrage. Yet you feel pressured to pick sides. *At least I'm not that kind of Christian,* you assure yourself. *I'd never attend that church with the sign out front that says, "Stop, drop, and roll doesn't work in hell." Or that church across the street promoting a "50 Shades of Grace" sermon series.* Body piercing may have saved your life, but you let your actions and not your T-shirts do the talking.

Even so, it's not enough to disagree privately. You need everyone to know your disgust for whatever those bigoted/compromised/know-it-all Christians said this time. How dare that man on TV claim to speak for God and you! Hell hath no fury like an embarrassed Christian.

We talk a lot about church unity. So where is the evidence that we actually want it? If you're anything like me, you're as much of the problem as the solution. You love other Christians so long as they make you look good to the world. You lament the divided church, yet you're quick to speak about the problems you see with other believers. You bemoan the church's ineffective public witness in a changing culture, yet you offer the same self-congratulatory solution to every new challenge. You find problems at the end of your pointed fingers and solutions in the mirror. In reality the finger pointed toward the mirror tells you where to search first for the problem.

We all have blind spots. It's so easy to see the fault in someone else or in another group but so difficult to see the limitations in ourselves. Unless you learn to see the faults in yourself and your heroes, though, you can't appreciate how God has gifted other Christians. Only then can you understand that Jesus died for this body, which only accepts the sick. Only then can we together meet the challenges of our rapidly changing age.

Maybe God has softened your heart with *compassion* for the broken, weak, and abused.

Or he has gifted you with great *courage* to stand with truth.

Or he has *commissioned* you with particular zeal and effectiveness to make disciples in all the nations.

God doesn't want us to look down on and suspect the worst of one another. Rather, he intends us to use these diverse gifts to love the world in a church united by the gospel of Jesus Christ. This moment demands our humility, bravery, and creativity. Why should the world know us by our disharmony, discouragement, and disillusion?

Never beyond Hope

As we point fingers at each other in the church, the world desperately needs our helping hands. Consider our predicament. We in the West learn from a young age that we're happy only if we're free to choose our life adventure. So we trust no one and commit nowhere. Until we turn to Christ, we worship nothing more sacred than self. And we have no greater goal than to be personally healthy and wealthy.

Thankfully, the gospel speaks to every age, including one with no higher aspirations for life than the freedom not to need anyone else except on our guarded terms. And God makes you, Christian, an ambassador of that good news: we can be reconciled to our Creator and live at peace with one another.

Rather than see us as ambassadors of peace, much of the world views the church as oppressive and self-interested. As a result, religious authority has been displaced, despite two millennia of Christian formation that gave shape to nearly every hope and right the West treasures. The new reality can hardly be considered an improvement. The world wonders why our social ties have frayed. Why neighbors don't look out for each other. Why couples don't want to get married and don't stay together when they do. Why we're plunging into demographic crisis as we wait so long to have children and then stop at one. Why corrupt, ineffective politicians think shouting at each other on news programs will solve problems. Why businesses subsume ethics to the bottom line. Why revolutions depose one despot to replace him with another. Why media promise leisure but leave us nervous and bored with yet another reality TV show intended to make our lives seem somewhat tolerable by comparison. Why our children feel the need to look and act like porn stars if they want to feel affection.

The picture looks bleak. You see it every day in your neighborhood, on the TV, and on your favorite websites. Christians dare not gloat over such suffering. We share in both the responsibility and the effects. We can relate to this disenchantment, because we're tempted even inside the church to see life in terms of control and power. We, too, fear everyone else is out to get us by limiting our freedom. We can't escape the culture wars.

Compelled by gospel love, however, we ambassadors of Christ know how to negotiate a truce—that is, if we'll first lay down the arms we've taken up against one another.

This book aims to help you see where perhaps you've gone astray and how to reorient yourself to follow Jesus and love your neighbor. Let's start small. Can you love a fellow Christian who sins differently than you do? That shouldn't be hard. You've confessed sin. You know you fall short of the glory of God (Rom. 3:23). Now let's get specific. If you live in an affluent area, do you regularly spend time with Christians tempted by laziness and gluttony? If you live in a middle-class neighborhood, can you identify close friends who confess their greed and arrogance?

If not, you may not understand the significance of God's forgiveness of your sins, and you may neglect to point others to find that same forgiveness by believing the gospel. This good news unites you as family to someone who may seemingly share nothing else in common with you except humanity. And the gospel creates an alternate community that reminds the world how much we all share as we bear the image of God.

What a contrast this gospel offers to the world! Everywhere we see the need and longing for community. On this planet we've never been more closely linked together due to our social media, volatile climate, massively destructive weapons, and multinational corporations. To live together peacefully and in prosperity we need basic consensus on what makes life well lived. True community shares a vision for the kind of character we want to cultivate in our children. But you can't even count on such agreement these days at your local PTA meeting or Little League game.

By the grace of God we Christians can show the world a better way. Jesus is our guide. He tells the truth about the world. And he gives life to all who ask. When his followers rest together in the love of a long-suffering God who does not share his glory with another, we can give up the fight for our reputation and get on with the work of the kingdom. Even now you can enjoy fellowship overflowing from Father, Son, and Holy Spirit, who from all eternity have loved in perfect harmony. If this God is for us, who can be against us? And how can we be against each other?

Because of this gospel, we can see opportunity in the rubble. We can find hope in the ruins.

Already you can see encouraging signs of this counter-revolution of grace. In your Christian community you can almost certainly find youthful zeal to love your neighbors near and far in practical ways. Look hard enough and you'll see new churches that love their neighbors and welcome the stranger to hear about Jesus. You'll see Christians standing courageously against injustice and telling the good news about Jesus at great risk. You'll enjoy artists and musicians who beautify our world to serve our creative God. Our heavenly Father forgives our finger-pointing and forbears our foolishness. With Jesus we're never beyond hope.

Three Responses

So that we don't squander that hope, you and I need a new narrative to understand our debates in the church and engagement with the world. Since at least the late 1800s and early 1900s, American Christians have been preoccupied with the battle between fundamentalists and modernists. This struggle has sought to situate Christians along a spectrum where they tend toward one side or the other. Depending on your perspective, modernists either update Christianity as necessary for a changing world or sell out the fundamentals of the faith for popularity. As for fundamentalists, they either defend Christianity in a hostile world or consign their neighbors to judgment. You could try to make peace in the no-man's-land at the middle of this battle, but that only means both sides shoot at you as they aim for their enemies.

I can't muster much sympathy for the modernists, whose project has destroyed the very churches it has purported to save. When you lose the distinctive doctrines of Christianity—starting with the resurrection of Jesus—you lose everything. But I reject the narrative that offers only these two solutions to our problems. And I resent the skepticism that pushes Christians toward one pole or the other. Consider the outcome as we look back on this battle for the soul of Christianity. The fundamentalist/modernist war left a legacy whereby, in some churches, you're branded a liberal heretic if you take away their hymnals. And in other churches a minister will sooner marry a man and his avatar than allow you to cite Ephesians 5 at a wedding.

As I survey the contemporary evangelical church, I now see three main responses to the world. You might use different names to describe them or even add additional characteristics—you could claim, for example, that a fourth group prioritizes "experience" of God over any other virtue. I have aimed to root my analysis in Scripture but don't claim that my three categories cover everything important to the Christian life. Rather, with an eye toward the limitations of the earlier fundamentalist/modernity divide, I want to show that none of these responses on its own reflects the depth and breadth of the way Jesus taught and the apostles followed. We tend to cluster around Christians with similar personalities, who reinforce our strengths but turn a blind eye to our weaknesses.

Many Christians are like me: we grew up in stable communities with strong extended families. We went to church because that was the right thing to do. We honored authorities and tradition because we believed they safeguarded the ways of wisdom. So if you're like me, you tend to see the church's problems as a failure of *courage* to walk the time-worn paths.

But a lot of Christians have different stories. If you scraped by in childhood and suffered abuse from leaders who should have protected you, you may see *compassion* as the great need of our day.

And if you've been weaned on the power of technology to effect needed change, you might think the only thing hindering unprecedented church growth is our resolve to fulfill the Great *Commission* through creative new methods.

None of us is entirely wrong. But you and I tend to reason from the personal to the universal and judge each other for our different experiences and perspectives. For every illness you see in the world you write the same prescription. And I do likewise, only with my preferred cure-all solution. Then you and I turn against each other in the church when we don't get our way. The problem is, we tend to separate what God has joined together. And he put you and me in the same church to build up one another according to our different gifts (1 Cor. 12:7). He wants to illumine our blind spots so we can see our differences as opportunity.

Where, then, do you fit in this description? Fill in this blank: The greatest problem with the church today is _____. Ask yourself, *Where do I invest the bulk of my time, money, and other resources?*

God variously calls us to champion certain causes. Such differences should be celebrated where we see them in our local churches, among evangelical churches in the same city, and even across movements of Bible-believing churches. Don't be concerned about "single-issue Christians," those believers with particular passion to end abortion, relieve poverty, adopt orphans, or close the 10/40 Window by sending missionaries to unreached people groups. Even if you don't share their interest or gifting, you can pray for them, support them, encourage them. But look out for "only-issue Christians," those believers who don't just want your help.

They demand you to fall in line behind their agenda. They do not tolerate other priorities.

You can learn to decipher between God-given difference and sinful divisiveness. Here's how you know you're divisive: you thank God you're not like those theology-obsessed fundamentalists. Or those bleeding-heart liberals. Or those pragmatic megachurch pastors. You already know the enemy before you know the details. You know the solution before you even know the specific problem. Furthermore, you don't pray *for* these opponents in the church. If anything, you pray *against* them.

But Jesus himself told us to pray for our enemies. Can you do so? Can you understand that different approaches may be needed in different scenarios, like a counselor exercising discernment and care? Even better, can you admit that we need all the compassionate, courageous, and commissioned Christians we can muster to work together out of respect for God's gifting and in obedience to Jesus? The magnitude of our challenges today ought to dispel the illusion that any one wing of the divided church can go it alone.

We need new hero stories. Or at least we need to vary the tales you and I tell each other to explain the solution for our problems. Think about the biographies you'd find on the bookshelves for each of these three groups. If you're *compassionate* you cheer the prophet who dares speak truth to oppressive authority on behalf of the wounded. If you're *courageous* you celebrate the lone warrior, bloody but unbowed by popular sentiment. If you're *commissioned* to reach the lost for Jesus you look up to the creatives, the influencers, the entrepreneurial leaders who leverage new measures for greater results.

In isolation these stories can conceal as much as they reveal. You and I suffer from a curious case of self-blindness. Only one Hero is above critique. Only one Hero is an infallible guide in every circumstance. Following Jesus warns us not to think every challenge demands the same solution. Sometimes you must shed a tear. Stand your ground. Brainstorm a fresh approach. Indeed, the example of Jesus reveals that our problems often compel all three responses at the same time. And the best way to respond faithfully and effectively is to lock arms with someone who sees the problem from a different perspective, who meets the challenge with a different skill set while staying faithful to Jesus above all.

Unless we shine light onto our blind spots and measure ourselves against Jesus, we will be tempted to apply our standards inconsistently.

The *compassionate* struggle to empathize with their critics.

The *courageous* don't like truth that makes them look bad.

And *commissioned* Christians don't always enjoy the mission when it jeopardizes their lifestyle and preconceived notions about the way of the world.

Instead of representing Jesus in all his wisdom, we're tempted to cast him in our own image. Having manipulated Jesus, we wield our chief concern like a stick useful for beating up other Christians who don't understand the problem.

35

Unfortunately, those other Christians often hit back. They don't see things your way.

Meanwhile, no one sees the bigger picture. Each stick is like a side of a triangle that represents either the heart, the head, or the hands of Jesus. Together these sides form the fullness of God's testimony to the world. Remove any side of the triangle and the whole edifice collapses into a pile of sticks useful only for beating.

Please understand: I'm not telling you to search for the perfect balance between heart, head, and hands, or compassion, courage, and commission. I'm telling you that if you want to follow Jesus in this world, you need all three in full, blessed abundance—in ourselves, our local churches, and the church at large.

The problem with blind spots is that they tend to hide behind good traits. Your weakness is often the flip side of your strength.

If you're compassionate, you sense your neighbors' needs. Good! So did Jesus. But you can be so concerned with what others think that you shrink from telling the truth, especially about Jesus.

If you're courageous, you stand fast in the face of pressure. Good! So did Jesus. But you probably fail sometimes to hear and heed legitimate criticism.

If you're commissioned, you look to explain the good news in a way the world can understand. Good! So did Jesus. But you also may struggle to confront the culture's values where they conflict with the gospel.

No mere attempt at "balance" can avoid the offense of the gospel. That's not the call of Jesus. But in aiming toward Jesus you and I can learn more precisely *when* and *how* we must offend as we put on his righteousness and put off our sin. Only by loving Jesus more than he loved the world could Paul distinguish between times when he needed to confront other Christians for undermining the gospel (Gal. 1:6–10) and when he rejoiced to know that other Christians preached the gospel even with mixed motives (Phil. 1:15–18). Neither situation should become our only paradigm for handling disagreement. His intimate grasp of the gospel made Paul jealous to guard it and eager for anyone to spread it. You would not describe him as balanced, as if he mixed a dash of tough love with a touch of free love. Instead, Paul loved Christ more than himself, so he feared neither criticism from false teachers nor suffering for righteousness' sake. He could be equally zealous for pure doctrine, generous charity, and urgent evangelism.

Better Together

Because of these blind spots, neither you nor I see everything clearly. We need each other. And hopefully by the end of this book you'll learn to see these differences as opportunities to serve Jesus more faithfully. You may also see that the same blind spots that apply to us individually plague many of our churches, blogs, and conferences as we tend to congregate around like-minded leaders. As a leader in one such ministry, I see this problem in myself and many good friends. And in this book I'll probably be harder on myself than others, because I'm more familiar with those temptations. I fear that spending time only around whatever group we regard as the "forces of light" can often make us all at least two-thirds blind. Rather than provoke judgment, your differences should primarily help me test whether I'm missing anything about the character of Jesus. Bravery, empathy, and innovation are all good and necessary because they roughly correspond to Christ's roles of prophet (courage), priest (compassion), and king (commission).

As the head of the church, Jesus guides us in how and when to respond in the proper role. You won't always excel in every capacity. But by learning to respect how God has gifted others, you'll enjoy God's power at work in your weaknesses. You'll grow in love and charity even as you deepen your convictions in God's good plan for the church in the world. You'll see that in the body of Christ, the head needs the hands needs the heart. Remember, we're not just looking for balance, as if we can triangulate the proper approach. The church needs you to bless the rest of us with your particular gifts so that together we're stronger when serving a needy world.

In the following chapters we'll explore how compassionate, courageous, and commissioned Christians can work together to meet the challenges of our age. We'll identify our God-given motivations and personality, appreciate these gifts as they correspond to the ministry of Jesus, illumine our blind spots, and consider how each of us makes a vital contribution to the church and the world.

The church of Jesus is the only institution equipped in this age of skepticism to enjoy unity in diversity through profligate, never-ending truth in love. Together as we notice our blind spots, we'll prepare to turn from our sins, follow our Savior, receive his reward, and await his return. We'll find evidence that the kingdom of God has already dawned in Jesus Christ. We'll search for signs that his kingdom advances in, through, and despite us. And we'll find hope for our time in the sure promise of a day coming soon when united we'll stand before the throne of grace.

2

Compassionate

New media have made it impossible for us to ignore the needs of the world. Your heart bleeds with news of another school shooting, another tsunami, another warlord on the loose. So you do what you can to help. You text ten dollars to the Red Cross. You change your Facebook profile picture. You buy a wristband. You tweet a #hashtag to topple dictators.

You have compassion in abundance. You clothe the homeless, feed the hungry, nurse the sick. You write the letters, shame the offenders, protest the powers.

You worry about the future of the church. Maybe you've seen your parents and pastors screw up Christianity. They've abused authority, failed to live out what they believe, and blamed everyone but themselves for what's wrong with the world. You're tempted to just walk away. But maybe you caught a radical vision of God's costly love for the world. So you stay in the hope of seeing renewal and reform.

Your compassion and zeal put you in good company with

Jesus. When you read the Gospel of Luke, you can't help but notice how Jesus always seemed to seek out the "little people." Zacchaeus was "small in stature" (Luke 19:3) but materially rich because of his job as chief tax collector in Jericho. When Jesus called him down from the sycamore tree, he welcomed this man joyfully, despite the grumbling of the crowd who resented Zacchaeus for cooperating with the Roman occupiers and exploiting the Jews. "He has gone in to be the guest of a man who is a sinner," they said of Jesus (v. 7). Actually, that was Jesus's mission—to find and befriend sinners so that he might deliver them from their bondage. "Today salvation has come to this house, since he also is a son of Abraham," Jesus told Zacchaeus. "For the Son of Man came to seek and to save the lost" (vv. 9–10).

Indeed, these "little people" were much more likely to respond favorably to Jesus's call than were the usual suspects of religious leaders. But Jesus tried to befriend the Pharisees, too. In fact, he was eating in the home of Simon the Pharisee when a sinful woman from the city anointed Jesus's feet with oil and wiped them with her tears. When Simon objected, Jesus pointed out that she had been much more gracious and hospitable than he had! "Therefore I tell you," Jesus explained, "her sins, which are many, are forgiven—for she loved much. But he who is forgiven little, loves little" (Luke 7:36–50).

We can't miss his message: compassion flows from understanding the magnitude of Jesus's forgiveness, won for believers on the cross and secured in his resurrection.

Born Blamers

Yet with every talent comes a temptation, with every strength a weakness. With compassion comes blame. In a broken world that lacks simple solutions and people who care, it can become all too easy to blame those who aren't mending our society. Compassion abounds for humanity, just not for humans.

Awareness of our own sin is the first step to compassion. But that's not where we usually start. Ask yourself this question: *Whom do I really hold responsible for the evil that befalls us?* Is it God? That columnist you hate? The other political party?

We live in an age that demands results. It's not enough to just listen and sympathize. Comforting the widow doesn't bring her husband back. Holding the orphan doesn't bring mom home. Compassion doesn't guarantee change. So we tend to channel our compassion into anger. We look for someone to fault. Everyone relishes a scapegoat.

We were born blamers. No matter how old you get, you can always blame your parents for how you turned out. Growing up we're convinced God gave us brothers and sisters so we'd have someone to blame. We know where to point the finger. We know who started the fight. She did it! It's his fault! Our common parents, Adam and Eve, started the trend. When God searched for Adam in the garden of Eden, Adam hid in fear because he had disobeyed God's command. When confronted, Adam shifted the blame. "The woman whom you gave to be with me, she gave me fruit of the tree, and I ate" (Gen. 3:12).

We're no different. Sure, you can admit that you're not always right. At least theoretically. No one since the garden is perfect, after all. But one thing you know for sure: the other guy is wrong. And even if he turns out to be right, you'd still rather be wrong in principle than cave to such a person. You imagine your adversary as having no redeeming qualities, no moral compass, no ounce of compassion. Everything becomes red or blue. Black or white. Fox or MSNBC.

But when anything or anyone but Jesus molds the shape of our compassion, we risk crafting love in our own image. The resulting idol of love leads us to make unintentionally destructive decisions based on false hopes. Take, for example, the strange promise you sometimes hear from those who see lack of compassion as the greatest problem with the church today. They argue that our compassion can win the world's favor. So when we sell our stuff, save our schools, and serve the suffering, we won't make enemies.

To be sure, I admire, even applaud, this optimism that Christians can make a difference with such intractable problems as global poverty and maybe even earn some respect and admiration in the process. And if they mean only that our good works will silence fools (1 Pet. 2:15), then I can agree.

But I do not believe Christians can ever win over the world this way. And when we expect that our good works should earn the favor of unbelievers, we're tempted to blame ourselves or especially our theological adversaries when the

Western world grows more hostile toward the church. We have enough jeremiads that place the sins of the world at the church's door. But even if we did more, gave more, and loved more, many would still reject us and the gospel Jesus preached.

If Jesus is our example in compassion, why did the world hate him and his apostles? The world, of course, put him to death along with most of his disciples. Jesus told us the world would hate us for loving him. He warned his disciples, "If the world hates you, know that it has hated me before it hated you" (John 15:18). The church must follow Christ's command to love our neighbors whether or not we ever receive thank-you notes. We will occasionally suffer antagonism for heroic stands on behalf of the most helpless among us—the unborn, for example. And in such cases we must know that the reaction of our neighbors cannot dictate our agenda. Compassion won't always be appreciated or even received by a world that rejects the source of our compassion.

Nothing Vain

The world will sometimes reject Christlike compassion, because our neighbors think the goal of life is happiness. And they understand that happiness primarily as freedom to choose. They cannot imagine a world other than one where they're free to live where they want, love whom they want, act how they want, buy what they want, and leave when they want. Right or wrong is just another preference. To limit choice and judge another's choices are the only universal wrongs.

The American Declaration of Independence has enshrined the pursuit of happiness as our right in life. And each one of us claims the right to pursue happiness in our own way without interference. Indeed, the logic makes sense: if this world is all we have, then there is no greater goal than to achieve happiness through freedom to choose.

If your neighbor asked, "What is the purpose in life?" how would you respond? Now try to answer again without Christian jargon. It's not easy. So how do we exercise compassion in a world that doesn't recognize godly compassion and may reject it? Truly compassionate Christians cannot simply accept the world's understanding that it needs happiness and freedom to choose. For the sake of our neighbors, we must question whether this path leads to true happiness.

If as a Christian you can't help your neighbors see the folly of this culture, then your compassion cannot truly help them. None of us can be happy if we seek in ourselves, in our choices, or in someone else the hope for peace and prosperity we can find only in God. And in such an environment we'll never escape the culture wars, because if there is no greater authority than our intuitions and needs, then there is no common ground for compassion. We can't even agree on how to love one another.

When you and I worry less about what the world thinks of us and more about what God wants for the world, then we'll have something unique to give to the world. Compromise in the name of compassion is a dead end. It's the quickest path to irrelevance. What starts out prophetic eventually ages into parody. What starts out defending the weak ends up using the same abuse tactics wielded against the weak: pressure campaigns, intimidation, and appeals to majority rule. Time and again I've seen the nastiest attacks delivered for the sake of compassion on behalf of the oppressed. So have you. And it's nothing new.

"Where oppression does not completely and permanently break the spirit, has it not a natural tendency to produce retaliatory pride and contempt?" C. S. Lewis asked in *Surprised by Joy*. "We reimburse ourselves for cuffs and toil by a double dose of self-esteem. No one is more likely to be arrogant than a lately freed slave."[10]

And, I might add, no one is less likely to see his arrogance than someone who lashes out from hurt. We must not confuse such a destructive response with compassion.

Jesus Wept

Only Jesus could correctly look at the world and not see himself as the problem. Yet his example shows us sinners how to see our blind spots and show genuine compassion. Some of us tend to weep over this lost world. Others seek indignant demonstrations against injustice. Jesus did both. In fact, Luke's account juxtaposes Jesus weeping with compassion as he looked at Jerusalem (Luke 19:41) with Jesus cleansing the temple in righteous anger (Luke 19:45–46).

Compare Jesus's example to how you react, for example, when you hear about young girls trapped in sex slavery. Should you weep over their plight? Or should you loudly and publicly protest this cruel injustice? Yes.

Our response gets more complicated, however, by sins not acknowledged as such in the world. Should we provide material and emotional assistance for women so they'll be less likely to choose abortion? Or should we denounce men who would rather pay a small hospital bill to get rid of their children instead of supporting them and their mothers? Yes. True compassion demands both responses.

We have such compassion on sin because we see the devastation. And if not us, then who? Christians seem to be among the only people to notice our social suicide. But we tend to see it in personal and predominantly sexual terms. We often fail to confront systemic sins. Just try to talk to your white friend about how the game of life has been rigged against ethnic minorities, especially African-Americans. These sins, too, demand weeping and gnashing of teeth. In our limited understanding we wring our hands over same-sex marriage but fumble over what to do about declining marriage and birth rates, the inequity of capitalism, and expensive wars that seem to have emboldened the spread of Islamic extremism in democratic guise. We bemoan personal, private evils such as pornography and sexting but offer no broader agenda for how we might disrupt the supply. Are we helpless to make a difference? Do we have nothing to say to the ghetto beyond "Here's some cash" or "Get a job"? Can we not find common cause to address war, gang violence, education, immigration, poverty, and much more?

Christlike compassion compels us to care about a wide range of evil, whether personal or social. But we can't solve these problems alone. So Christians will need allies who don't agree with us on every issue. In the aftermath of the Religious Right, these allies will trust us only if they can see and hear our compassion and do not fear that we have an agenda to impose our values on an unwilling populace. Before acting on your compassion, ask yourself this question: *How do my neighbors know I care for them?* In other words, *What does my compassion cost?* Your neighbor is more likely to listen if you have skin in the game. Think of the difference between decrying violence in a neighborhood 25 miles from your house and wailing over a child from your block lost to a stray bullet. When the bullets are flying, you can hear only the voices of friends huddled next to you in the trenches.

I learned about my own lack of compassion the hard way as I got caught up in complex societal sin. When the housing market collapsed in the United States, I shook my head at neighbors who borrowed more than they could afford and lost their homes to foreclosure. My wife and I lived within our meager means. We made the prudent decision to buy at a time when home ownership promised safe returns. I criticized government efforts to save my neighbors from their mistakes.

Then I tried to sell my home. And nothing happened. In fact, I learned that my house was worth a fraction of what we had paid seven years earlier. Government and markets create winners (people trying to buy a house in 2010) and losers (people trying to sell a house in 2010). I started to understand how banks eager to expand profits failed in their responsibility to adequately screen loan candidates. And they had the audacity to conspire with the government to portray such irresponsibility as compassion. Through no fault of my own, I lost much of what I had saved for a future home. I earned little money as a magazine editor, and I had no way to make up the difference.

For a long time I did not respond to my hardship by following Jesus and loving my neighbors. I raged against the banks. I complained about the government for making the problem worse with a homebuyer tax credit that seemed cruelly timed to expire just before I decided to sell. I sank deeper into anger and despair when the only promising buyer bailed on us. What should have aroused compassion for others in the same situation, especially my overwhelmed real estate agents, only made me more suspicious and resentful of them.

The whole sordid affair should have taught me that only God can be trusted to love me patiently through every circumstance. I dare not expect salvation from government, from the markets, or even from my good decisions and planning. None of these can address my fundamental needs and desires, my hopes and dreams.

Only after the fact could I understand how Jesus shows me the time to weep and the time to rage. Even my neighbors who made bad decisions deserve my compassion as human beings made in the image of God. Yet we also live in a fallen world where all of us, from buyers with poor credit to bankers with rich portfolios, need restraint and accountability as fellow sinners. Compassion will sometimes look to the world like licentiousness as we extend grace. And sometimes it will look like hardship as we tell the truth about human nature in bondage to sin from birth.

Lasting Peace and Prosperity

True compassion weeps for the world. "My eyes shed streams of tears, because people do not keep your law" (Ps. 119:136). But by God's power we can do more than weep for the world. Weeping turns to praying, and praying turns to helping. You and I are the means God employs to lavish compassion on his creation. You may not have the financial means to express the depth of your thankfulness to God and love for your neighbors. But generosity is measured in more than money (2 Cor. 8:12). In fact, it's possible to give your cash and not yourself. Compassion can be expressed through hospitality, time, and attention. So retweet that article on sex trafficking. Even better, look in your own neighborhood for immigrants and refugees who may struggle to fit into their new home. Trust God to open your heart with compassion for immediate neighbors, and he'll certainly fill you with love for your global neighbors.

I'll never forget the charge R. Kent Hughes, longtime pastor of College Church in Wheaton, Illinois, delivered shortly before he retired. He told our prosperous suburban congregation not to forsake our commitment to countercultural generosity. We devoted nearly half our budget to missions in our community and around the world. We welcomed our neighbors struggling with disabilities to worship among us and sought to meet their physical and spiritual needs. Church members opened their doors to refugees and immigrants learning English and other skills needed to survive and eventually thrive in the United States. My friends visited prisoners and opened their homes to ex-convicts looking to start over as new believers in Jesus Christ. Apart from this generosity of energy, time, and other resources, Hughes warned us, we could gain the world and lose our souls. Indeed, I learned that my response to the poor reveals my grasp of the gospel. If I remain indifferent to the poor, how can I say I understand the unmerited favor of God in saving me from my sin?

"The gospel opens our eyes to the fact that all our wealth (even wealth for which we worked hard) is ultimately an unmerited gift from God," The Gospel Coalition's Theological Vision for Ministry explains. "Therefore the person who does not generously give away his or her wealth to others is not merely lacking in compassion, but is unjust. Christ wins our salvation through losing, achieves power through weakness and service, and comes to wealth through giving all away."[11]

The world can ignore another special-interest group. They can ignore another awareness campaign. They can even ignore another law. But the world cannot ignore churches united around this vision, Christians who put this compassion into action. We don't even need a political majority to act. Consider the example of the civil rights movement. If you've never learned what it's like to be in the minority, now is the time to prepare. Start your research with this momentous period.[12] You can do justice, love kindness, and walk humbly with God even if you can't claim an ally in the White House.

But like every other movement for justice, we'll need to realize it's easier to unite around a common enemy than to advance the common good. After defeating their enemy, movements suddenly notice their intramural differences and turn on each other. They lose sight of the justice of their cause and feed on internal conflicts as various voices angle for market share and control.

Genuine compassion must compel you to forsake this path so many peers have taken. It won't make you popular. It won't likely attract attention. No one will be able to squeeze you into their preconceived notions. You won't fit neatly in any one camp, even when you learn from them and appreciate their particular contributions. But you won't stand apart from others in pride, either. If Paul could give thanks for those who preached the gospel out of ill motives, we can do the same. He understood the sin that lurks in the dark recesses of every heart. He knew no one would have pure motives until Jesus returns and takes away our love of sinning. Until then we'll disappoint—probably our neighbors, certainly ourselves. Somehow, though, God's grace will be enough. Somehow the treasure of the gospel, stored in human jars of clay (2 Cor. 4:7), will testify to God's power. And somehow he will finish the good work he started in us (Phil. 1:6).

Longing for the coming of God's kingdom sets us apart from the world and also from other Christians who trust themselves and expect too much from this age. Until Jesus returns, all the compassion we can muster cannot resolve world hunger, war, and poverty. Sometimes these problems may worsen; other times they will improve. Thankfully the God who sends rain on the just and the unjust alike (Matt. 5:45) has gifted us with the resources to make some progress. We can foster a just and humane society by aligning our public policies according to the knowledge that God has made all of us in his image, and yet we all suffer the effects of the fall.

To be clear, our goal is not to eradicate evil altogether. After all, the only way to eliminate evil is to eliminate you and me. And even then the creation would groan under sin (Rom. 8:22). In fact, if we expect to liberate the world from injustice, we promote the legalism of impossible expectations. This kind of compassion helps no one and destroys us in the process. Not until the world has been finally renewed through Jesus Christ and fully glorified in the new creation will we enjoy lasting peace and prosperity.

What's Wrong with the World Today?

In the meantime, consider the attitude of G. K. Chesterton, the great twentieth-century British writer. The story is told that the *Times* of London once asked several famous authors the question, "What's wrong with the world today?" It's a question we continue to ask ourselves with the best compassionate motives. Chesterton responded to the *Times* inquiry,

Dear Sir,
I am.
Yours, G. K. Chesterton.

The apostle Paul might have answered similarly, if I understand his first letter to Timothy correctly. The foremost New Testament author was the self-described foremost sinner (1 Tim. 1:15). We read his list of former demerits: blasphemer, persecutor, insolent opponent (1 Tim. 1:13). But we rejoice with him that "the grace of our Lord overflowed for me with the faith and love that are in Christ Jesus" (1 Tim. 1:14). And we might even imagine putting our arm around him and saying, "Cheer up, Paul. You're not so bad. We all make mistakes." But his wording in 1 Timothy 1:15 is emphatic: Jesus came to save sinners, he says, and I am the foremost. As we listen, stunned, we imagine Paul insisting, "You don't understand. No one hated the church more than I did. And I proved it: going door to door, dragging out followers of Jesus, and approving their execution. I even thought I was serving God by killing them."

"Well, I've never done anything that bad," we respond, tugging on our shirt collar as the room seems to warm. "Maybe you're right, Paul."

But Paul doesn't let you and me off the hook, either.

Remember, Jesus didn't come for the healthy. He came for the sick. If we want the grace that overflows in compassion, then we'd better get in line behind Paul and Chesterton. What's wrong with the world? Blame me.

When your compassion expresses itself in finger-pointing, you're supposing your understanding of the world roughly corresponds to God's. But consider this: Paul once thought he was loving God by hating Jesus. He thought the most compassionate thing he could do for his community was to kill Christians. He celebrated the crucifixion as God's good judgment against a blasphemous criminal. He knew the good guys from the bad guys and acted on that conviction to protect his loved ones.

How could he be so wrong, so deluded? Paul had spent his whole life studying God. No one had more religious confidence. As to righteousness under the law, he was blameless (Phil. 3:6). But when God stood before him in the flesh, Paul didn't recognize him. Can you imagine? Be careful, then, about trusting your conscience. The heart is deceptive. Paul didn't feel sick. He thought he was cleansing Israel of sickness by attacking the church.

How can you be sure you're not wrongly judging others right now in the name of compassion? Here's a quick gut check: if your sin is somehow less deserving of judgment than someone else's, you're in trouble. Paul wrote in Romans 2:1, "For in passing judgment on another you condemn yourself, because you, the judge, practice the very same things." Who hasn't been on the other side of this judgment? Even in a world that rejects God's authority over right and wrong, we still relish separating the good from the bad. Just try saying you don't recycle. Or that you smoke. Or that you can't find time to exercise or the willpower to diet. The responses will not be compassionate.

You'll often hear that Christians are judgmental. And it's true that when the church claimed to speak on behalf of a moral majority, we failed to understand that our judgments did not strike the minority as compassionate. But this is not a problem just for Christians. All of us share the temptation to scapegoat in the name of compassion. Now that the church represents a minority view on issues such as gay rights and religious liberty, we fear that our enemies want to exact revenge. Tolerance sounds like a good idea until you have the power to enforce your morality. The heart is never so deceptively cruel as when convinced of its purity.

So how do we escape this cycle of recrimination? As Christians we believe in moral authority more than majority rules. We believe only genuine compassion conforms to this standard set by God. How do we reveal to the world that we follow a better way that leads to truth and life? Consider what changed with Paul. What made this sin-sick man well?

Paul met Jesus on the road to Damascus, and God gave him a pure heart. But the apostle used a curious phrase when he explained his transformation in 1 Timothy 1:12: Christ Jesus our Lord, he says, "judged me faithful." But how did God make this judgment that made Paul faithful? So far as we know, Paul didn't confess his sin when he saw Jesus.

He didn't beg for his life. He didn't even promise, "I'll never do it again!" But his silence before the risen Jesus pled ignorance and his need for mercy (1 Tim. 1:13). So the grace of God completely overflowed for him in faith and love. That same compassion would overflow through Paul to others during countless trials and while suffering in prison until his death in Rome.

This was a curious judging that made Paul faithful. Until this point Paul hadn't been faithful in anything but violent zeal against the church. Nevertheless, God judged him faithful to serve him as an example for anyone who wants eternal life. The life and ministry of Paul tells us Jesus Christ alone is the source of perfect patience and compassion.

Think about those you want to blame for the problems in the world. Can God make such an example out of them? And if God can be patient with you, can you be patient with them? Even those you fault for their lack of compassion? What would happen if you stopped judging others and started judging yourself chief of sinners in need of God's grace?

This is incredible: Paul tells his story in the context of warning young Timothy, pastor in Ephesus, against false teachers. He's not afraid to judge between good and bad teaching, even by naming names (see 1 Tim. 1:20). Twisting the gospel is blasphemy against God and cruelty toward your neighbor. It sends people to hell. Nothing could be more important to Paul than guarding the gospel.

Yet as he stood courageously for the gospel, Paul never

got over grace. He even made up a word in 1 Timothy 1:14 translated as "overflowed." As God's grace overflowed to him, he overflowed with gratefulness. He met Jesus, and he understood what Jesus meant when he said the first would be last (Matt. 19:30) and that the meek will inherit the earth (Matt. 5:5). He would follow this Jesus even to the ends of the earth. And in doing so he shows us how to have compassion on our neighbors.

Only when you judge yourself a sinner will God judge you faithful.

Only when you confess your disobedience will God make you an example for others seeking eternal life.

Only when you understand God's mercy toward you can you extend mercy to others.

Only in your ignorance can God make you wise to salvation.

So what's wrong with the world? I am.

And how does God change the world? How does he show compassion? He sends Jesus to meet us in our ignorance and entrusts us with the good news that even great sin cannot defeat so great a Savior.

3

Courageous

We honor our heroes by giving them the key to the city. By naming a school after them. Maybe we even name an entire day after them. Courage is treasured by any of us who watched New York City firefighters rush into the burning World Trade Center towers shortly before they collapsed.

Courage is not the only virtue extolled by Christians. But as with training to become a firefighter, it's essential to fulfilling the rest of our job description: to love, to serve, to rebuke, to evangelize, and so on. Without courage you cannot love the unlovely. Without courage you cannot discipline your children, tell your friend she's making a destructive decision, or say no to temptation. Without courage you cannot talk about Jesus with those who don't yet have ears to hear.

If God's Word and history teach us anything, it's that you don't become a Christian because you want to be popular. Or remain popular. Mayors didn't give Paul the key to their cities. He was more likely to flee the murderous crowds under the cover of night. Courage took Jesus to Gethsemane, to Calvary, to the tomb. Christian courage comes from knowing that the worst this world can do is get rid of us. As the Puritan Richard Sibbes once put it, "They can kill us, but they cannot harm us." God never abandons his children. Yahweh told his servant Joshua:

> No man shall be able to stand before you all the days of your life. Just as I was with Moses, so I will be with you. I will not leave you or forsake you. Be strong and coura- geous, for you shall cause this people to inherit the land that I swore to their fathers to give them. Only be strong and very courageous, being careful to do according to all the law that Moses my servant commanded you. Do not turn from it to the right hand or to the left, that you may have good success wherever you go. This Book of the Law shall not depart from your mouth, but you shall meditate on it day and night, so that you may be careful to do ac- cording to all that is written in it. For then you will make your way prosperous, and then you will have good success. Have I not commanded you? Be strong and courageous. Do not be frightened, and do not be dismayed, for the LORD your God is with you wherever you go. (Josh. 1:5–9)

When Paul commands us three times in Ephesians 6:11–13 to take up the whole armor of God, he also tells us to "stand." It's a common biblical image for courage. And it's a common theme in church history, too. The great Reformer Martin Luther picked up on it when he refused to budge from his conviction about the gospel as revealed in God's Word. Whether he spoke these actual words or not, they testified to his costly courage: "Here I stand, I can do no other, so help me God." In our own day the controversial young president of The Southern Baptist Theological Seminary, Albert Mohler, appealed in his first convocation address to the school's confession and charged hostile faculty and students, "Don't just do something, stand there!"

Maybe the most countercultural thing you can do today is stand firm and stay put. Not change your mind. Not assume newer is better. Not back down when under pressure from the world. John the Baptist's head ended up on a platter. Jesus hung on a cross. Stephen succumbed to a hail of stones. Following God requires courage. Indeed, Jesus fully expected that some who pose as Christians would lack courage and succumb to the world. He explained in his parable of the soils, "As for what was sown on rocky ground, this is the one who hears the word and immediately receives it with joy, yet he has no root in himself, but endures for a while, and when tribulation or persecution arises on account of the word, immediately he falls away" (Matt. 13:20–21). Courage is necessary for us to endure in the faith.

The example and teaching of Jesus, along with that of his followers, show us precisely how Christian courage differs from the world's. We don't expect accolades. And neither do we needlessly provoke for selfish gain. Jesus was silent before his accusers (Isa. 53:7; Matt. 26:63). Paul said we should rather be wronged than defend ourselves from every accusation (1 Cor. 6:7). Followers of Jesus show compassion for sinners even as they suffer.

Imagine yourself today in a Nigerian village harassed by marauding Muslims. The most courageous thing you can do in the face of murderous persecution is to continue loving the enemies who killed your family. Confidence in God's ultimate judgment allows us to stand strong and show mercy even under great duress. As Paul told the church in Corinth:

> So we are always of good courage. We know that while we are at home in the body we are away from the Lord, for we walk by faith, not by sight. Yes, we are of good courage, and we would rather be away from the body and at home with the Lord. So whether we are at home or away, we make it our aim to please him. For we must all appear before the judgment seat of Christ, so that each one may receive what is due for what he has done in the body, whether good or evil. (2 Cor. 5:6–10)

Courage will not necessarily appear bombastic. Often it will look more like quiet confidence. If Christ is coming back to judge the living and the dead, you and I don't need to overreact to the ups and downs of each day. Evil laws and popular heretics will come and go, but the Word of the Lord will stand forever.

Fog of Nostalgia

As with compassion, however, courage comes with its corresponding temptations. Because courageous Christians expect opposition, it's easy to court it with brash arrogance. And because we feel so strongly about our convictions, we sometimes defend secondary and even tertiary concerns as if they are matters of life and death. Consequently, we're prone to pessimism and diagnose disagreement as dangerous compromise. We're always the heroes in our own stories of standing athwart history. We long for an earlier, less complicated, less compromised era.

But in reality every generation thinks of its own era as a watershed. They think the days have never been so evil, the challenges never so big, the times never so urgent. So the moment demands extraordinary courage. We circle the troops for one last stand.

There's only one problem with this view. Every generation seems to forget that history doesn't look so kindly on last stands. One man's hero is another man's fool. Even Custer was popular in his time.

You and I are more like our ancestors than we want to admit. We hear that this new idea, new law, or new technology will change everything—for better or worse. Alarmism makes for a good fundraising pitch. It calls forth the best and the worst of human nature. It preys upon our deepest fears that everything we love can be lost. And sometimes it draws out our latent courage so we resolve not to take these threats lying down.

I worked in political fundraising, and I saw this principle in action. Fear is a more powerful motivation than hope. It's easier to stir hate than love. And when you can stoke enough hate, you can build a potent campaign to elect your candidate or advance your cause. You never need to explain what your candidate will do if you can scare people into fearing the alternative. Everyone complains about negative advertising, but no one would spend the money if it didn't work.

Christians can succumb to this cynical view of the world, too. Among those who say courage is the biggest need of our day, you don't hear a lot about hope, despite its prominence in Scripture. Hope is a blind spot for us courageous Christians. We fear the future and bemoan our times. We tend to measure our age against the past and wish we were born in a different day. But remembering the past, contrary to what we often tell ourselves, does not always bolster belief in the present. Why? Because nostalgia is the enemy of faith. We assume courage will result from doomsday threats as we contrast today's troubles and our faithful forebears. Instead of courage, though, we get despair. By lamenting the good old days, nostalgia tempts us to forsake the present day as beyond the scope of God's redemption, out of reach from his intervention. And when we venerate the saints of yesteryear as titans of faithfulness, without paying proper attention to their sins, we elevate them to a status only God possesses. As they increase in our memory, God must decrease. Even Jesus seems unfit to tie the sandals of some of our heroes.

Flawed Followers

Thankfully, Scripture shows us what proper veneration looks like for our courageous heroes. We can indeed learn much from these men and women who stood strong in the faith when many others abandoned the gospel. Real courage, unlike nostalgic cynicism, doesn't pretend anyone is perfect. Even our heroes' mistakes help us learn courage from their examples.

I love studying Peter, whose courage was so legendary that he's said to have been crucified upside down in Rome. If Jesus had wanted to rule God's kingdom in force, Peter would have marched on Jerusalem at his right hand. It was Peter who stepped out from the disciples and first confessed Jesus as "the Christ, the Son of the living God" (Matt. 16:16). And it was Peter who believed his courage would compel him to stand by Jesus and die even if all the others fell away (Matt. 26:33, 35).

This same Peter, moments after his boast, couldn't even stay awake one hour as Jesus prayed in the garden of Gethsemane and waited for his betrayer to come (Matt. 26:40). And, of course, this same Peter emphatically denied Jesus when two servant girls and a crowd of bystanders recognized him as a disciple of the Galilean (Matt. 26:69–75). He felt anything but courageous as he wept bitterly that evil evening.

But even when Peter's faith failed, Jesus remained faithful. The other disciples didn't believe the women who told them an "idle tale" about two angels at the tomb. They explained Jesus had risen just as he told them he would on the third day after being delivered into the hands of sinful men. Peter, however, didn't waste time doubting but ran to the empty tomb to see the good news for himself (Luke 24:1–12). Everything changed for him that day, because he learned that

Jesus is the same yesterday, today, and forever (Heb. 13:8). He finally understood that God demonstrates his power by working through flawed followers.

But this Peter, who once cowered before servant girls, later stood before the Jewish ruling council and defied their warning not to speak or teach of Jesus. Along with John he answered, "Whether it is right in the sight of God to listen to you rather than to God, you must judge, for we cannot but speak of what we have seen and heard" (Acts 4:19–20). The council couldn't understand such courage, such disobedience from uneducated, common men. They couldn't see that the resurrection changed everything. But Peter had been cut to the heart by a message he knew would turn the world upside down.

The Bible never shies away from depicting Peter in all his vulnerability. We see him at his best and at his worst. Even after his courageous stands at Pentecost and before the council we watch him misunderstand the implications of the gospel for Gentile believers not circumcised according to Jewish law (Gal. 2:11–14).

You will not insult your heroes to suspect their imperfection. Rather, if you ignore their mistakes, you'll insult their God and cloud your faith with the fog of nostalgia. Your own day will never measure up by comparison. Instead of inspiring courage, your heroes will make you doubt you can measure up to their lofty standard.

Nostalgia doesn't do subtlety. It pounds the third dimension out of our heroes, turning them into cardboard cutouts suitable for display at our favored conferences. You can't so much learn from these heroes as deploy them in contemporary arguments. In doing so we dishonor their legacy and forsake a great opportunity to humbly appropriate their God-given strengths and seek to avoid their inevitable weaknesses.

Truth is more complicated than memory. It's also more reliable. If we remember our heroes for who they were—sinners redeemed by a glorious Christ—we'll gain courage from their example and deepen our faith in a God who can powerfully work through us, too, even in this wicked day.

Prophetic Posture

As we see in Peter, the only kind of courage that will sustain us in truth and love comes from our identity as sinners saved by grace. When you forget that you need your courageous, prophetic message about Jesus as much or more than anyone else, your courage appears to others as mere arrogance.

Courage to repeat the same old failed approaches is foolishness. Being hated by the world doesn't necessarily prove you're courageous. You speak boldly about marriage and abortion. Good! Now devote the same courage to fighting racism and averting war. The church has not always done so, and the consequences have been devastating for both the church and the world. Don't be surprised if the world prefers a bad solution when we offer no solution.

Courage is more than countering the culture, more than saying no to the world. We pray for those who persecute us. We love our enemies. We seek their prosperity, now and especially forevermore. But if they can't see the compassion in our courageous stands, we appear to them as just another power-grabbing interest group. If you don't communicate in a way your neighbors can hear, you may not love them so much as you enjoy the satisfaction of rejection. Courage may in fact be your blind spot.

Consider this: what have you done to make your church a welcoming place for neighbors not like you? You may criticize churches that have adopted the cultural idiom and downplayed the fear of God. But invite your neighbors who don't normally attend church and see your church service through their eyes. What isn't explained? Who isn't introduced? What words need translation? Remember, we want unbelievers to contend with the foolishness of the cross, not our religious jargon. If they leave confused, don't pat yourself on the back thinking, *They just can't handle the truth.*

Let's get even more personal. What sins are publicly confessed in your church? Consult a list such as Galatians 5:19–21. Maybe your church talks often about sins such as sensuality. Do you also seek forgiveness for strife? Envy? Rivalry? We cannot simply dismiss the world's dismal view of the church as evidence that we're living faithfully for Jesus. Outsiders see our churches as more than content to baptize a conservative utopia where government punishes other people's sins and doesn't touch our freedom, consumerism, and inequality. They think we're in it for ourselves. They don't see Christianity as caring for the world. They don't see how faith in Jesus makes any difference for everyday problems such as lack of access to quality education and job opportunities. We talk about religious freedom, and they hear us pleading for special privileges. We talk about conversion, and they hear us recruiting new Republican voters. We talk about courage, and they hear us pining for the black-and-white 1950s.

If you're like me, you typically blame the world for not understanding. That's a blind spot for us. You're tempted to say good riddance to a world that has always rejected the prophets and suppressed the conscience in sin. Claiming to be wise, the ungodly exchange the glory of the immortal God for idols and become fools (Rom. 1:22–23). And to some degree, you're right. We don't expect the world will necessarily recognize our courage as love. We know that genuine compassion is not possible apart from courage to defend biblical doctrine. Yet in sin the world rages against the heavenly Father, even though he always knows best. That's the biggest problem with working toward the "common good," as nice as that phrase sounds. What if the world doesn't want what is good for them?

Unfortunately, when opposed by the world, we courageous Christians tend to succumb to pessimism. We defend the doctrines of grace without grace and confuse rejection of us with rejection of Jesus. But Jesus didn't give up on his foolish disciples. He even forgave his murderers from the cross. And he didn't give up on you and me in our sin. So pessimism doesn't make us heroic. Courage that counts makes you faithful in whatever place and position God has given you. This courage makes you fervent in spirit, patient in tribulation, and constant in prayer as you serve the Lord with zeal, always rejoicing in his sure hope (Rom. 12:11–12). And the challenges we face in a changing world will weed out all but the fervent, patient, constant, and rejoicing Christians. Pessimism and retreat will not suffice.

Sick Sinners

Until recently in the West, Christianity demanded a particular brand of courage to resist holier-than-thou stereotypes. Criticism of Christians tended to highlight either naïveté or hypocrisy. Think about the kind of Christians you see on television. Which role do you fit? You could be a goody-two-shoes rube, most likely from the Midwest or South, like Ned Flanders from *The Simpsons* or Kenneth Parcell from *30 Rock*. Or you could be a judgmental hypocrite like *The Office*'s Angela Martin, who would take only the Bible and *The Purpose-Driven Life* to a desert island but still sleeps around with her coworkers.

You need courage to persevere in love when those you meet typecast you in one of these unfortunate roles. Journalists don't often help, either. It's usually not news when Christians serve soup to the homeless. But it's always news when a church leader misappropriates benevolent funds for personal gain. The world resents our moral standards and gloats over our failings. Somehow we've perpetuated a myth that depicts us as the worst of both worlds: moral superiors in public but deviant hypocrites in private.

The world thinks we're attracted to Christianity so we can judge others according to a strict morality issued by a harsh God. So we're seen as counterrevolutionaries who seek to turn back the clock from the tumultuous 1960s to the supposedly stable 1950s, from an era of free love to a time of costly conformity.

But the days ahead will require a different kind of Christian courage. You can already see the stereotypes shifting. No longer will the world try you for hypocrisy. Instead, you will be charged with bigotry, our culture's worst sin. You will be judged and convicted for intolerance. No longer suspected of false moral superiority, you will be accused of real moral inferiority. The revolution is victorious, and retribution is coming. Rather than Victorian prudes, evangelicals have already been likened to Jim Crow segregationists for opposing gay marriage.

To much of the world this new era looks like a tolerant utopia. But as Christians we know we can never discount the human ability to justify ourselves through "moral" living. We're all tempted to think better of ourselves by looking down on someone else. We judge one another as immoral for not using the right lightbulbs. For not buying organic. For voting against the anointed candidate. For sending our children to the wrong schools. For eating the wrong fast food. For buying the wrong shoes. For watching the wrong shows.

Whether you admit it or not, we all live by a moral code

that rewards certain behaviors and punishes others. If you're a Christian, that code should correspond to the Bible. At least you can look up the laws and cite chapter and verse. For many others, the new morality shifts under your feet with the rise and fall of new Internet memes. One day you'll chuckle at a celebrity's crazy antics. The next day you'll shake your head when you learn he checked into a drug rehab center. One day you'll laugh at the wide receiver knocked silly by the hard-hitting safety. The next day you'll mourn the linebacker who took his own life after suffering too much head trauma while delivering those blows. You don't know what the new morality will bless and condemn with each new day. You just know there will be something to bless and something else to condemn. The rage machine never breaks down or loses power.

As ever, courage will be crucial in this new era. And godly courage will demand that Christians withstand this pattern of retribution and refuse to respond in kind. This will be a hard habit to break. Conservative Christians have wielded the power of "majority rules" politics when it's suited our purposes. Indeed, Christians sought to roll back the excesses of the 1960s when the "silent majority" backed Richard Nixon in 1968 and 1972. As a result, we became associated with a corrupt political machine that escalated an unjust war. And the world rightly wondered whether we proposed to turn back the clock on hard-won civil rights for African-Americans. Following a brief time of regrouping after Nixon's presidency collapsed, the Moral Majority resurrected to bolster Ronald Reagan in 1980 and 1984. Many of us got what we hoped for in George W. Bush, who identified as a born-again Christian. But after his unpopular second term ended in 2008, the pendulum swung far away from his "compassionate conservatism."

Even when winning some political battles, Christians lost the culture in America. Now we can't even win the political battles. There is no going back. There is nothing left to recover. There is no majority to recover it anyway. There must be a better way to demonstrate courage and not leave the impression that God's Word is an oppressive moral code for strange people who find solace in a judgmental God.

No New Challenge

Indeed, there is a better way. Our situation does not differ altogether from the challenge endured by early Christians in the Roman Empire. By the standards of state religion, deemed essential to secure divine favor and battlefield victories, Christians were regarded as sacrilegious. Romans did not see Christians as naïve or hypocritical. They saw this strange new sect as unholy, a challenge to the authority of the state, enemies of the gods, a threat to social unity and well-being. So emperors, particularly the infamous Decius in AD 250, imposed mandatory pagan sacrifices designed to divide and conquer the small but growing Christian community. Though many Christians succumbed to the persecution—whether by death or by capitulation—the church grew in stature and number.

Why? We can see at least two reasons. First, the accusations simply didn't match the reality. In the letters between Roman rulers about how to handle these Christians, even these ruthless men admitted that followers of Jesus care not only for each other but also for their neighbors. The government might treat Christians as enemies of the state, but for the abandoned child nursed by faithful women, or the man restored to health by patient caregivers, Christians were friends of humanity.

Second, the Roman way of life had begun to collapse as Christianity spread throughout the empire. Barbarians threatened the capital city. Morale and morals declined. Hope dimmed. Some Romans blamed Christians and their strange Galilean religion. But many more saw in Jesus a greater savior than Caesar, a better teacher than Cicero. Christianity explained their world better than any alternative.

You and I today face nothing approaching the threats endured by early Christians. We marvel at these resilient heroes, memorialized in the remarkable testimony of martyrs such as Cyprian of Carthage. But we don't worship the martyrs. Do we not, though, worship the same God? Do we not read the same Scriptures? Do we not follow the same Jesus?

We are not the moral majority. You and I are sick sinners saved by grace alone so that we cannot boast. And we cannot remain silent about what we've seen and heard. We proclaim good news about a Savior who wants more than morality from us. We will not abandon the political process, because that's one way we love our neighbors. Sometimes we'll seek to enact and enforce laws that serve the common good, even when the world protests. How? We'll need to continue learning from the most effective Christian political movement of the last one hundred years. The civil rights movement won over skeptical allies and eventually even entrenched enemies without abandoning their trust in God's law.

We'll need such wisdom and savvy, not to mention courage, as we ask God to help us work for justice and mercy in this fallen world. We'll need to build and join diverse coalitions to fight against sex trafficking, abortion, education inequality, and many more problems that plague us. You probably don't need to know a principal's views on gay marriage in order to respond to her plea to mentor students who lack godly role models. You don't need to agree on gender roles in the church to work with an agency to deliver women held captive to satisfy men's carnal urges. And you don't need the same view on universal health care to pass a law that protects helpless children in their mothers' womb. Real courage values making a difference over merely appearing courageous in defeat.

Father, Forgive

This courage flows from humility, because heaven will not ratify any of our agendas without amendment. We'll need the leading of the Holy Spirit to know when and how to take a stand. In prayer we'll need God to help us discern our priorities. His voice must ring louder in our ears than the bombast of talk-show hosts. The Bible reliably guides us toward the clearest teachings. And history counters our biases by exposing us to the experience of wise believers from other cultures in different times.

All the while, charity must guide our dealing with other believers as we remember that everyone matures in faith while learning from God in his perfect timing. Courage is not measured by how many people you can offend. So be careful not to suppose you can divine someone else's motivations. How much does your nemesis on Twitter really know about you? That's roughly the same amount you know about him or her: not much. Tread carefully, then. Only when you argue with your opponents at their best can you truly love them even in disagreement. Godly courage demands nothing less.

When someone treats you as an enemy of humanity for siding with God, return kindness for insults, "so that, when you are slandered, those who revile your good behavior in Christ may be put to shame" (1 Pet. 3:16). As Jesus once commanded Peter, put down your sword so you don't win the battle and lose the war (Matt. 26:52). Never argue unless you can demonstrate the fruit of the Spirit: love, joy, peace, patience, kindness, goodness, faithfulness, gentleness, self-control (Gal. 5:22–23). This way, you might actually have a chance of persuading someone who disagrees.

A couple of stories from the man who defines courage may help us understand how to love our neighbors without losing our conviction. Jesus taught the Pharisees a parable in Luke 18 about a persistent widow so that they would pray and not lose heart. In other words, he wanted them to take courage and trust God despite the troubles of the world. So he told them about a judge who respected neither God nor man. This widow, obviously not in a position of social or political strength, would not stop pleading her case before him. "Give me justice against my adversary," she demanded (v. 3). The judge didn't care at all about her case. But he didn't like being annoyed. So he gave her justice. The widow was rewarded for her courage.

You can probably see Jesus's point. If this judge granted justice to a widow he didn't even love, how much more does God desire to do justice on behalf of his elect when they cry out to him for help? "He will give justice to them speedily," Jesus explained (v. 8). We have courage, then, not because we trust in our own wisdom or strength but because we trust in a God who loves his people and delights to show it. Courage does not calculate the odds; it appears odd to the world because it trusts in deliverance from another world.

Even as we learn about courage from Luke 18:1–8, we must see how the next story, Luke 18:9–14, informs that understanding. In this parable about the Pharisee and the tax collector, Jesus intended to expose how some trust in their own righteousness and treat others with contempt (v. 9). As we've already discussed, this self-righteousness is always a temptation for those of us who see ourselves as courageous. Jesus explained that these two men entered the temple to pray, but their prayers exposed vastly different hearts. The Pharisee prayed, "God, I thank you that I am not like other men, extortioners, unjust, adulterers, or even like this tax collector. I fast twice a week; I give tithes of all that I get" (vv. 11–12).

Meanwhile the tax collector couldn't look up. He was too ashamed to even gaze in God's direction. As he pounded his chest he cried out, "God, be merciful to me, a sinner!" (v. 13). This man, like Zacchaeus, had betrayed his people. He'd compromised to serve the foreign ruling power. No doubt he'd taken advantage of his authority to exploit his own neighbors. But this man and *not* the law-abiding Pharisee, Jesus taught, returned home righteous before God. "For everyone who exalts himself will be humbled, but the one who humbles himself will be exalted" (v. 14). No wonder the Pharisees regarded Jesus as immoral, as a threat to their way of life, and conspired with their enemies to put him to death.

You and I tend to measure courage by faithfulness to a moral standard or by intellectual assent to a historic creed. But based on what Jesus taught and how he lived, we're telling only part of the story. Courage cannot be separated from humility, grace, compassion, or love. Courage can look like John the Baptist denouncing Herod for taking his brother's wife. And it can look like the Master kneeling to wash his disciples' feet. According to Jesus, humility precedes exaltation. In fact, no one will enter the kingdom of God except those who receive it like a child (v. 17).

Genuine courage develops not only when we study the Bible and fight for truth but also when we pray, when we pass through the waters of baptism, when we take the Lord's

Supper, when we enjoy the fellowship of the body of Christ as a member of a local church. Courage, finally, is not so much something we do for God but something we humbly receive from him as a gift. And if it belongs to us as a gift, then it's something God intends for us to share for the good of others.

4

Commissioned

Liven up your next gathering of friends by asking them why young adults stop going to church or never attend in the first place. Even if your conversation partner has never been to church and thinks of Trinity as the movie character he had a crush on about fifteen years ago, he'll still venture an opinion. You don't need to know much about Christianity to think you know why people these days reject it.

Church-attending Christians, too, relish the opportunity to speak their mind. Do you worry that traditional churches aren't relevant to everyday experience? Think they're boring? Do you complain that church people are unfriendly and the pastor can't relate to you? Maybe you believe the next Jesus movie could be the great cultural breakthrough we've longed to see. Or you urge churches to adapt the most innovative technology for online congregations and multi-site venues so they can reach people who wouldn't consider walking into a traditional building. If these objections and suggestions sound familiar, you might be a commissioned Christian.

You might be a commissioned Christian if you worry that younger generations will slip away or never bother to show up unless churches adapt to changing times. You're not exactly conservative or liberal in theological terms. You probably trust in the authority of Scripture and hold to conservative views on issues such as the exclusivity of Christ; otherwise why bother with evangelism? But you don't fit in with Christians who actually enjoy debating theology or arguing over whether ministry practices conform to Scripture. You want to get on with the serious, urgent work of changing lives with the power of the gospel.

As a commissioned Christian, you fit comfortably within the mainstream evangelical movement, at least in the United States. You may be a young believer who pledged to follow Christ as a high school student or a new parent who found spiritual refuge in megachurch, but you can trace your spiritual heritage back to the origins of evangelicalism in America. Evangelicals, being Christians concerned with renewal, have always worried about complacency in the church, especially among the younger generations. Such angst convinced New England Puritans in the 1600s to adopt a "half-way covenant" to accommodate the children of parents who could not claim credible conversion experiences. Even these stalwart Christians worried the church would lose its cultural standing unless they lowered the barrier to belief.

Still today you can travel the two-lane roads of the Bible

Belt and drop in on a sweat-soaked revival sermon to hear a terrifying warning against backsliding. And every summer you can drive from Christian music festivals in South Dakota to camps in Upstate New York to escape from the cares of the world and reinvigorate your relationship with Jesus. From the piney woods of Alabama to the toll roads of suburban Chicago, you'll hear that the world needs Christians serious about their commission from Jesus: "All authority in heaven and on earth has been given to me. Go therefore and make disciples of all nations, baptizing them in the name of the Father and of the Son and of the Holy Spirit, teaching them to observe all that I have commanded you. And behold, I am with you always, to the end of the age" (Matt. 28:18–20).

These words spurred Baptists and Presbyterians to bring good news to the rough and independent American frontier during the late 1700s and early 1800s. They inspired missionaries to shove off from the safety and security of England for the malarial jungles of Africa and Asia. They prompt a college student today to walk across the cafeteria to talk with a stranger about Jesus. Belief that the Great Commission still applies to us today separates evangelicals from churches that have sued for peace with our pluralistic age.

If you're a commissioned Christian, you know that we cannot simply expect neighbors to show up in church. We cannot even expect that our own children will feel obligated to carry on our religious traditions. Actually, we never could. But the stunning church growth in the United States that preceded the Civil War and followed the Second World War bred a kind of complacency that is common to postrevival periods. Commissioned churches cannot be content with this status quo, because eternity is at stake.

While other Christians complain about the headwinds that thwart the advance of the gospel, commissioned churches charge right in. You're not intimidated by the open marketplace of ideas. You celebrate the absence of official religious establishment because it forces American churches to contend for resources and members. You understand that the logic of the consumer market prevails. If your church can't offer a compelling alternative to professional football, golf, or sleep, your church will end up like the mom-and-pop general store after WalMart moves to town. So commissioned churches experiment with new methods to spread the gospel at a time when we cannot assume a broadly Christian understanding of sin or framework for responding to the message of salvation.

If you're commissioned, you probably read and share articles and books about the rise of the "nones," especially young Americans who claim no religious affiliation. You're burdened to reach them for Jesus, even if you don't agree on the best way to do so. You're not likely to agitate for theological reform, whether reinvigorated orthodoxy or rebranded liberalism. You don't have time to ask why we got into this mess, and you see much theology as needlessly divisive. You're united by mission, and you claim no creed but the Bible.

Indeed, you might not even know about the regular fights that consume many Christians who live on Twitter. And why would you care? Your churches tend to dominate the mod-

False dichotomy

est skylines of small towns and suburbs across the United States. In a results-oriented culture, commissioned churches have found a formula that works. Few of us these days stick to the same denomination our whole lives, let alone the same local congregation. Almost all of us have shaken the dust that collected on our feet from the ugly red carpet at the dingy old church of our youth. Now our feet glide on the smoothly polished basketball gym floors of the elementary school that hosts our church plant or the multipurpose auditorium of our megachurch.

Seek and Save the Lost

I don't always see eye-to-eye with commissioned Christians, especially when theology takes a backseat to practice. But I respect and even admire how commissioned Christians see opportunity in situations other believers would dismiss as hopeless. In one rural area I know well, a young pastor defied traditional religious leaders to start a new congregation in a town that didn't seem to need one. But he saw that all the other churches were in decline and had no plans to welcome the shrinking number of young adults who hadn't moved away for jobs and other opportunities. So in his early twenties and without much education or experience, he planted a church that borrowed ideas from what he'd seen work in other towns. Within a decade he led the largest and most vibrant church in town. That's what God can do with a commissioned church.

When I was far from God, commissioned Christians sought me out and introduced me to a Jesus I had heard about in church and Sunday school but scarcely understood. I didn't know what exactly these Christians believed, but I could see they loved Jesus. Their love showed me there must be more to Jesus than I ever expected.

By reaching out to me, commissioned Christians simply followed the example of Jesus, who likewise came for them "not to be served but to serve, and to give his life as a ransom for many" (Mark 10:45). Through their persistent love I learned that I was a lost sheep pursued by the Good Shepherd (Matt. 18:10–14; John 10:11). As they taught me how God had come for me, they encouraged me to go to others with this good news.

Under this influence in my early years as a believer, I rejoiced over the apostle Paul's description of Jesus's incarnation. He came to us at the appointed time and place, in human flesh, and made himself nothing so we could become children of God.

> Do nothing from selfish ambition or conceit, but in humility count others more significant than yourselves. Let each of you look not only to his own interests, but also to the interests of others. Have this mind among yourselves, which is yours in Christ Jesus, who, though he was in the form of God, did not count equality with God a thing to be grasped, but emptied himself, by taking the form of a servant, being born in the likeness of men. (Phil. 2:3–7)

Paul didn't just study these concepts in preparation for writing these world-changing words. As the greatest missionary of all time, Paul lived out this calling as a commissioned Christian. He might not have been present with the disciples to receive the Great Commission, but he gave his life to fulfill it. No shipwreck, beating, or imprisonment could stop him from spreading the gospel. He refused to allow himself to be a stumbling block to the advance of God's kingdom.

> For though I am free from all, I have made myself a servant to all, that I might win more of them. To the Jews I became as a Jew, in order to win Jews. To those under the law I became as one under the law (though not being myself under the law) that I might win those under the law. To those outside the law I became as one outside the law (not being outside the law of God but under the law of Christ) that I might win those outside the law. To the weak I became weak, that I might win the weak. I have become all things to all people, that by all means I might save some. I do it all for the sake of the gospel, that I may share with them in its blessings. (1 Cor. 9:19–23)

That attitude compels commissioned Christians at their best to remove every obstacle to belief in the gospel. Whenever you first professed faith in Jesus, you can probably identify at least one Christian who sought you out and explained the good news in a way your faintly comprehending mind could understand. Maybe today you look back and wonder about the wisdom of that initial method of delivering the gospel. Maybe you think the message you heard lacked important elements. Even so, if you're like me, you owe an eternal debt of gratitude to commissioned Christians.

Positive and Encouraging

As we saw in earlier chapters, all strengths come with corresponding weaknesses, every gift with a blind spot. In this case of commissioned Christians, their search for cultural relevance can slide into syncretism. And their eagerness to expand the tent can culminate in theological compromise. Sometimes these churches don't merely resemble the mall with their expansive parking lots and food courts; they also communicate with "practical" and "relevant" messages that Christianity is an à la carte faith that supplements our private pursuit of peace, wealth, and status.

You might not always hear it in commissioned churches, but the gospel changes more than our salvation status and promises more than moral improvement. While we're promoting sermons about Faithbook and iPray, the world wants to know if we offer something better than personal health and wealth. When we treat our neighbors as consumers, they see us as peddlers. Without a distinctly Christian understanding of mission, we offer them nothing better than what they can find on afternoon TV or a therapist's couch. If your faith demands nothing, you will give nothing.

Carrying out the Great Commission in Western culture, you and I must lean on the Holy Spirit to resist the tempting allure of consumerism and individualism, even as we learn to understand these values. They aren't all bad; every culture enjoys common grace in some areas. You can explain a lot of the vitality of the church in the United States, for example, by appreciating the value of making faith a personal pursuit. And you always know that when one denomination surrenders to the spirit of the age, the Spirit of God seems to raise up another new fellowship of churches zealous to take the gospel into new and neglected markets.

But the Great Commission isn't great unless we obey everything Jesus commanded. And that means you need to, well, teach disciples to obey everything Jesus commanded. That takes time, discipline, and patience. In our microwave culture, however, we tend to teach disciples enough to warm them up for the waters of baptism. Once we can count them in the club, we turn them into recruiters. When we promote the gospel with the same methods perfected by Amway, we shouldn't be surprised when our neighbors treat Jesus as a tool that can be discarded when something better comes along.

Churches poised to please the culture with a pitchman pastor may think the world needs a more positive and encouraging message, maybe something safe for the whole family. Such churches may see Sunday morning as essentially an escape from the cares of the world, a security blanket for the huddled masses. But if you fall for this false promise, you will gain the world and forfeit your life (Mark 8:36). Your faith will dwindle to a purely private practice that does not compel anyone else to follow you as you follow Jesus. You will be safe from the world's scorn. But you will not have a gospel that turns the world upside down. You will not know the joy that compelled the disciples to defy the authorities of the greatest empire on earth and receive the kingdom that will not end.

You can't match Christianity to perfectly suit this age, because the market doesn't care about truth. Look at the most successful preachers on television. Few of them are successful because they have "knowledge of the truth, which accords with godliness" (Titus 1:1b). To gather a crowd today you don't need to preach God's Word. In fact, if that's your only goal, you probably shouldn't. You should smartly package together nice-sounding self-help platitudes with a sterling smile or a sassy sensibility. The masses refuse to believe in a God with any higher goals than our personal happiness. And plenty of churches seek to accommodate them and call it "mission." Their commission actually betrays a blind spot.

Unless you contextualize your mission with honest understanding of local culture, you merely add to the noise, because you will become accommodated to the spirit of the age. You'll think you just teach the plain old gospel, when you might actually share a compromised, diminished substitute. Your mission will be guided by practical considerations, but soon you'll learn "whatever works" is no sure foundation for faith in a turbulent age. You'll beg for relevant sermons that bolster your self-esteem, self-confidence, and self-improvement and wonder why your self doesn't change.

Care Is Cheap

The implications of misapplying Paul's missionary methodology are not just limited to evangelizing individuals. When you assume basic congruence between Christianity and culture, you become assimilated to agendas at odds with the gospel. Christians on both ends of the political spectrum have fallen victim to parties using them to grasp power. And that power has corrupted our gospel witness. In seeking to control the culture we've been controlled by the culture and bowed down to its idols of wealth and status. So now we're caught in the aftermath of a culture war we never should have waged with worldly methods. The Moral Majority's stand with the status quo falls flat in a fallen world. The counterculture is no better, for it promises freedom but delivers slavery to self.

Now should be a prime time for learning from our mistakes. Within the last decade every Christian in America, no matter his or her political persuasion, has been at some point overjoyed and another point devastated. Every Christian now has ample evidence to confirm God's Word: "It is better to take refuge in the LORD than to trust in princes" (Ps. 118:9). No political or economic system can enjoy God's blessings apart from God's law and love.

Instead I fear that evangelicals still think the right candidate or even new technology can secure a brighter future. But no new media or political platform can change the human heart. You cannot trust in any movie or stump speech to negate the need for the Great Commission. When we overpromise, we're tempted to overdeliver with results manipulated by human hands. If something sounds too good to be true, it might be. As I've heard pastor Ray Ortlund say, echoing Francis Schaeffer, it is evil to do the Lord's work in our own way. The hype machine rarely winds down quietly; it usually comes down in a crashing halt.

Here's the really sobering point: no one may notice at first if you seek to fulfill the Great Commission in your own power. You may appear successful, even admirable in the eyes of the world. Wealth and status may appear to you initially as tools to spread the gospel rather than temptations to forsake the way of weakness extolled by Paul (1 Cor. 1:18–31). Only in the long run will your failure of faith catch up to you.

Look at the burnout rates for pastors. Some fail because they lose their first love. Others fail because congregations pressure them for results, no matter the methods. I know many pastors who fell under the pressure to perform bigger and better shows each Sunday. They set the trap for themselves, because they trained Christians to think the gospel needs smoke and mirrors. If we're really following Paul's missionary example, the opposite is true: "My speech and my message were not in plausible words of wisdom, but in demonstration of the Spirit and of power, so that your faith might not rest in the wisdom of men but in the power of God" (1 Cor. 2:4–5).

If you must choose, it is better to fail in the eyes of the world than to succeed without the Lord.

Alienated from America

Despite the aforementioned blind spots, the outreach impulse of commissioned churches is necessary and encouraging. We need more of this entrepreneurial spirit. In the spirit of the marketplace, creative and innovative churches challenge other Christians in the same community to evaluate their own methods and traditions against the standard of God's Word and the urgency of the Great Commission. Pastors who enjoy reading and learning from a Steve Jobs biography can be powerful assets in the hands of God, provided that's not the only kind of book you'll find on their shelves.

But if we're hoping to unify Christians in the rubble of cultural catastrophe, only the original Great Commission handed down by Jesus can draw together the disenchanted but hopeful, the revolutionary but peaceable. We cannot confuse our mission with the pursuit of fame and fortune. If we can finally wake up from the American Dream, you and I can cast a vision of the sure and coming kingdom. Wealth and status in the world cannot compare to the "inheritance that is imperishable, undefiled, and unfading, kept in heaven for you" (1 Pet. 1:4).

In order to meet the challenges ahead and fulfill our missional mandate, we'll need less talk about practicality and more talk about humility and simplicity. We don't need to act as if Jesus needs our ingenuity. And we'll need to expect suffering. We need not fear, though, because Jesus sent a helper, the Holy Spirit, to guide us into all truth (John 16:13).

He goes before us and convicts the world concerning sin and righteousness and judgment (John 16:8). We do not, then, disciple in our own wisdom or power but baptize in the name of the Father, Son, and Holy Spirit (Matt. 28:19).

When the Spirit guides us into the truth of Jesus's teaching and convicts the world, we see how he confronts every culture, including our own. God creates us as individuals but not for ourselves. Contrary to popular belief, you will not find freedom in expressing your autonomy—only in obeying the Son for eternal life (John 3:36). Jesus lived among us, so he understands the cares of the world and the deceitfulness of riches (Matt. 13:22). In fact, the Devil led Jesus into the wilderness and tempted him by offering rule of the world's kingdoms and all their glory (Matt. 4:8). All he needed to do was fall down and worship Satan (Matt. 4:9).

The irony is that Satan promised Jesus something he could not deliver. And Jesus turned down something he already possessed. We learn from the apostle Paul that by Jesus "all things were created, in heaven and on earth, visible and invisible, whether thrones or dominions or rulers or authorities—all things were created through him and for him" (Col. 1:16). But "being found in human form, he humbled himself by becoming obedient to the point of death, even death on a cross" (Phil. 2:8).

If anyone wants the only wealth and status that last, then, Jesus shows the way. He reveals the way to be truly human. Accept limits. Give your life away. Seek personal fulfillment but only in loving others first. Find security in coveting the only treasures that rust cannot destroy and thieves cannot steal (Matt. 6:19–20). The good life can be summed up in these simple yet profound commands from Jesus: "You shall love the Lord your God with all your heart and with all your soul and with all your strength and with all your mind, and your neighbor as yourself" (Luke 10:27). These words have never stopped changing lives.

Tragedy and Tumult

Because Jesus walked among us, he understands the tragedy and tumult of life. We must not leave the impression in our worship services that Christianity offers escape from the trials of life, as if you can only worship God when smiling and clapping along to an upbeat band. A church that does not lament cannot teach new believers the way of Jesus.

Even Jesus wept when his friend Lazarus died (John 11:35). And his mission did not always make sense to even his closest friends. Jesus endured gossip from crowds about why he didn't intervene to save Lazarus, the grievous charge from Mary that her brother would not have died if Jesus had been around, and the faltering faith of Martha, who could not see the glory about to be unleashed in her brother's resuscitation. Jesus—the one who is before all things and in whom all things hold together (Col. 1:17)—then prayed aloud to his Father for the benefit of the people with thanksgiving that this miracle would reveal the Christ's divine mission. This act of mercy finally prompted the Pharisees and chief priests to conspire together to kill Jesus. Our Savior's whole mission reveals that God's power will not be overcome—indeed, it will be revealed—amid the tragedy and tumult of this world.

While our neighbors and even fellow believers suffer, you hear a lot from evangelicals about the need for practical sermons, practical books, practical articles. I would ask them: Practical for what? Practical for my wealthy suburban neighbors is not the same as practical for Egyptian Christians under attack from Muslim militants. Practical for a stubborn and selfish eighteen-year-old (been there) is not the same as practical for a thirty-five-year-old woman who welcomed with tears her first child, a stillborn son. Practical on September 10, 2001, is not the same as practical on September 11.

Truly practical messages equip us for life. They prepare us to suffer and die well. They commission us to speak the gospel into the darkest corners of our own hearts and on the dust-caked corners of Lower Manhattan. Jesus's arms extended on the cross hold together triumph and tragedy. At his moment of greatest agony, humanity broke free of our greatest enemies, sin and death. At our moments of greatest pain, the risen and ascended Jesus shows his greatest love.

Suffering intermingles with love in our fallen world being made new by Jesus. These seemingly opposite states of being actually coincide until Jesus returns. Think about how you reacted while watching the towers fall on that dreadful morning of September 11. I felt a strange sinking sensation in the pit of my stomach as the second building collapsed. And then I felt another new and unusual urge. I wanted to do something, anything, to help. In college at the time, I considered joining the military, something that had never before occurred to me as necessary or realistic. I recalled the contentious election less than a year earlier as I watched with awe and appreciation as politicians joined together to sing "God Bless America."

No one wants to relive that awful day. But we understand something about God and human nature when we remember how the same tragedy that reveals the worst of human nature simultaneously draws out the best of human desire for care, unity, and purpose. Our commission, then, must not ignore the dangers of the world and the evil humans can inflict on one another. Nor should we aim for practical messages that imply that faith should gratify all our personal wants and feelings. Unless we confront Western individualism and consumerism, we baptize values foreign to the kingdom of God and the teaching Jesus commanded us to obey. Pursuit of wealth and status has already sidelined too many Christians who started out zealous to fulfill the Great Commission and settled in, content with their personal prosperity.

Truly Good News

The only truly good news transcends every culture and translates into every culture. The one real gospel judges every culture and justifies in every culture. Use this standard to evaluate the church service you regularly attend or lead. Does congregational worship seem strange to outsiders, at least at first? Good, it should. You cannot expect everyone to walk in off the street and understand every word sung, preached, and read. The Great Commission does not negate God's other commands for how we honor him when we gather together.

At the same time, commissioned Christians help the rest of us see that there should be a loveliness to the strangeness, a friendliness to the unfamiliarity of congregational worship. Explain terms and introduce practices wherever possible. More importantly, let the light of the gospel shine in your interactions with one another, whether you're preaching from the front or watching infants in the nursery. You can't control how outsiders will react to the gospel, but you can remove yourself as a hindrance to belief. As the apostle Peter told the elect exiles of the dispersion, "Keep your conduct among the Gentiles honorable, so that when they speak against you as evildoers, they may see your good deeds and glorify God on the day of visitation" (1 Pet. 2:12).

You can't do better than 1 Peter to learn how the early church lived out the Great Commission under severe social pressure. Churches today spend months of deliberation and thousands of dollars to generate purpose or mission statements. If Jesus's own words from Matthew 28:18–20 don't suffice, save the time and money and borrow 1 Peter 2:9: "But you are a chosen race, a royal priesthood, a holy nation, a people for his own possession, that you may proclaim the excellencies of him who called you out of darkness into his marvelous light." Just try to improve on that rich theology and glorious purpose.

If coming generations prefer the darkness to this marvelous light, then we will mourn together. But I've learned too much from commissioned Christians about trusting in the sure and loving promises of God to give up on the church. Where we must change our music and methods to meet the times and welcome new believers, let us do so without selfish regard for our former ways. Where popular preachers tell us to compromise our beliefs, let us instead trust in the power of the gospel to advance in our weak and lowly condition. And where the world pleads for hope and for answers amid suffering, let us point to Jesus, "the founder and perfecter of our faith, who for the joy that was set before him endured the cross, despising the shame, and is seated at the right hand of the throne of God" (Heb. 12:2).

He is coming again soon. Until then he invites us to carry out the greatest commission he's entrusted to us.

5

The Counterrevolution Will Not Be Televised

So far we've discussed the Christlike traits of compassion, courage, and commission along with their corresponding blind spots. In light of that discussion, we now conclude by seeing these differences as opportunity by following Jesus in the fullness of each trait according to his example of abiding love.

Almost everyone loves something about Jesus. Some of us love his courage to endure the scorn and shame of the cross. Others love his compassion to associate with sinners and liberate the oppressed. Still more love his commission for the disciples to heal the sick and cast out demonic spirits.

It's harder, though, to love the real Jesus who does all this and more, then calls us to follow in his steps. We often seize on one aspect of his character and ministry and brandish it as a weapon against other believers. And we rope our partial Jesus into some of the nastiest conflicts.

There's hope for us, however. And we find it in unlikely places, such as God's faithfulness to the most dysfunctional church of the New Testament. The apostle Paul contended with a church torn apart by divisions and ineffective in its public witness due to the lack of distinctive gospel community. Based on reports, Paul's teaching about Jesus hadn't sunk in. Unity had been undercut in more ways than we can recount. Some got drunk while others starved at the Lord's Supper, and scandal inside the church made even outsiders blush: a man slept with his father's wife.

Factions had formed in Corinth, a proud city that loved strong personalities. But in this starstruck city that demanded signs and wonders and words of wisdom, Paul offered a stumbling block: Christ crucified for sin and raised from the dead according to the Scriptures. "For the foolishness of God is wiser than men," he told them, "and the weakness of God is stronger than men" (1 Cor. 1:25).

Paul didn't bother flattering the recipients of his letter. Not many of them were wise, powerful, or noble in the eyes of the world, he observed. But as he explained, "God chose what is foolish in the world to shame the wise; God chose what is weak in the world to shame the strong" (1 Cor. 1:27). God did this so that the church of Christ would display unity amid the diversity of spiritual gifts. When we believe, the Spirit unites us to Christ and to one another in the body of Christ, the church.

Let's assume you've made this confession. How do you know you believe it in your heart? Examine your life: do you associate with those who sin differently than you do? We all continue to fight the world, Satan, and the flesh. Do the people in your life tend to share the same strengths and weaknesses? Do you gravitate toward friends who have similar life experiences and outlooks on the world?

Say the Spirit has blessed you with a gift to discern right from wrong and good doctrine from bad. But in the flesh you're tempted to judge the doubting and hurting. Can you in unity with the body show them compassion?

Or you're the kind of person who gets things done. You're a fixer, a planner. You don't read a lot, and you're not the academic type. But you want to see the church grow and thrive. Can you slow down and show mercy to the vulnerable? Can you honor the theologians who pore over the Bible to help us know what it means?

Or you love the poor, the outcasts, and the abused. Good! Can you also love the bankers, the doctors, and the lawyers? Can you respect their vocations and urge them to live out their calling for the sake of Christ?

It's easier to associate only with our own. But anyone in the world can have that kind of community. You'll find it every Saturday afternoon in football stadiums. You'll find it in country clubs. You'll find it in any protest march. That's just community, not the variously gifted and blessedly eclectic community created by the gospel. True community results only from a miracle.

Paul names different parts of the body to underscore how God gifts Christians in different ways to build a vibrant whole. The foot needs the hand, and the ears need the eyes. If you have a discerning ear for truth, you need the eyes that see our neighbors in need of compassion. If you extend the hand of mercy, you need the feet that know when to flee temptation. Your courage didn't earn your salvation; neither did your compassion or your dedication to the Great Commission. Everyone doused with the Spirit has a vital purpose. The Spirit of life set us free in Christ Jesus from sin and death (Rom. 8:2). That Spirit who raised Jesus from the dead now dwells in all who believe (Rom. 8:11). He testifies that we belong to the family of God as heirs with Christ (Rom. 8:17). He has equipped you with just the talents, experiences, and desires you need to bless others (1 Cor. 12:11). You belong to the body God always wanted.

If the Spirit has gifted me with courage, then that same Spirit may have gifted you with compassion. Or perhaps he has gifted you with particular zeal to fulfill the Great Commission. I can't look down on you for being different, nor can I envy you for having the gift I want. God has a plan to unify us in our diversity.

You can clearly see from Paul's letter that the Corinthian church had a problem with elitism. But look carefully and you can also see how elitism birthed a related problem with inferiority. "The parts of the body that seem to be weaker are indispensable," the apostle observed (1 Cor. 12:22). In true gospel community you don't hang out only with other Christians who share your strengths. You don't congregate in homogenous units. You don't give greater honor to the rich, the outspoken, the powerful, the connected. You celebrate the weak, the lonely, the poor in Spirit.

Many politicians think soaring speeches make us love them. In reality, however, no flowery prose will make us love a mayor who can't get the snow-filled streets plowed and the garbage removed. The most beloved politicians make us long for a better world and support the people who can actually make it so. They know you get unity and purpose when you deflect honor and credit. That kind of unity makes people take notice and want to join. Paul taught us this much in a strange passage, 1 Corinthians 12:23–24, in which he said the body of Christ gives greater honor to the less honorable parts and treats our unpresentable parts with greater modesty. Essentially, we tend to treat the eyes and ears as the most important parts of our body. But we can live without them. Many parts of the body that we conceal are more essential to our survival. So it is in the church. The weaker parts more clearly demonstrate the power of God.

Let me offer one suggestion for where the church can chart a better course than the world in the power of the gospel. Our world distrusts authority. We assume leaders only want the best for themselves. To be sure, some leaders give us reason to doubt their sincerity and selflessness. Even in the church, leaders sometimes abuse their authority and shame their critics. But the Bible tells us God gifts some Christians as leaders. Authority is necessary to preserve unity, because the urge to divide is inevitable so long as we're in this fallen world. Our diversity of gifts is often the source of that division. You complain the church doesn't take advantage of your gifts; often you mean the church needs to reflect your tastes and preferences. I've been guilty of fostering this division. So how do we overcome such division and show the world a better way?

Say you see legitimate problems in the church. That's not surprising, because leaders are sinners, too, and they make mistakes. They will be much more likely to hear your complaint if you have affirmed and honored their gifts from God. And if they see you exercising your own gifts for the good of the whole body as you heal, help, teach, or anything else, they'll understand that your concern comes from love and not resentment. Authorities who listen and respond humbly to concerns stand out in this world. And so do the rest of us when we obey our authorities as God commanded (Titus 3:1).

The best part about this unity is that we don't need to earn it to prove ourselves to God. This unity already belongs to us as a gift. We are the body of Christ! We do not just aspire to 1 Corinthians 12. This vision belongs to you and me in Christ by the Spirit. So as a family of faith we suffer with the suffering. We rejoice with the rejoicing (1 Cor. 12:26). You enjoy gifts from God so you can use them to love one another. Don't look down on anyone with the weaker gifts. Don't judge someone with different strengths. If nothing else, remember that 1 Corinthians 13 follows 1 Corinthians 12. If you're the courageous type who gets annoyed by compassionate and commissioned Christians, then God's love should move you to bear all things, believe all things, hope all things, and endure all things (1 Cor. 13:7). Christ first loved you not on the merits of your strengths but in spite of your weaknesses. Give God the glory for bringing unity from our diversity of spiritual gifts. And when he gets the glory, you'll get the joy of a gospel community that appeals to the world.

Biblical Fullness

You don't achieve the kind of ministry fullness Paul advocated by aiming for fullness. You achieve this biblical fullness when you aim for Jesus. No one ever called Jesus "calculated." Rather, he is the Savior named Faithful and True who will return on a white horse (Rev. 19:11). In the meantime he left us powerfully direct words that guide us in following him in faithful and true ways even in a daunting world.

The next place we turn to for hope is another unlikely place—the setting where Jesus identified his betrayer and predicted his most faithful disciple would deny him at his hour of greatest distress.

During this Farewell Discourse, recounted in the Gospel of John, Jesus told his disciples that unless we "abide" in him we can do nothing (John 15:4–5). His words must have stung his confused disciples; they still sting us today. "If anyone does not abide in me he is thrown away like a branch and withers; and the branches are gathered, thrown into the fire, and burned" (v. 6).

No one wants that result, so what does it look like to "abide" in Jesus? We don't commonly use that word today, so we need to look at the context of Jesus's teaching to understand. First, we see the wonderful result of abiding in Jesus. "If you abide in me, and my words abide in you," he says, "ask whatever you wish, and it will be done for you" (v. 7). When we abide in Jesus, we enjoy such close fellowship that we pray the kinds of prayers he delights to answer. He gives us wisdom, peace, and patience in abundance.

Second, we see the condition of abiding in Jesus. "If you keep my commandments, you will abide in my love, just as I have kept my Father's commandments and abide in his love" (v. 10). This is a daunting standard! Who, then, can hope to abide in Jesus? Even if you avoid breaking God's laws against lust, envy, and sloth, you can hardly hope in your own willpower to "love the Lord your God with all your heart and with all your soul and with all your mind" (Matt. 22:37). You need a supernatural love, a love that transcends our fickle moods and mortal flesh. You need love from above: "Greater love has no one than this," Jesus explains, "that someone lay down his life for his friends" (John 15:13). This abiding love took Jesus to the cross to pay the penalty for our sins. It triumphed over death in his resurrection. And it intercedes even now on our behalf as the ascended Christ sits at the right hand of the Father.

This love belonged to all who believe even before Jesus created the world with his Father. It certainly did not depend on the disciples' performance or foresight to follow him. "You did not choose me," Jesus told his disciples, "but I chose you and appointed you that you should go and bear fruit and that your fruit should abide, so that whatever you ask the Father in my name, he may give it to you" (v. 16).

Abiding in Christ is the best defense against the blind spots that destroy our joy in following Jesus and set us against other believers with different gifts and callings. Abiding in Christ will protect you from growing discouraged and getting sidetracked in trying to obey Jesus's commandments. Some people you try to love will reject you because they have rejected him. Some Christians and churches suffering from blind spots will fault you for not caving to their pressure. You see this discord where the world presses for conformity from the church. Western culture's idol of sexuality tempts churches to respond in limited, even self-destructive ways when beset by blind spots. Some withdraw in fear from the world and call it courage. Or they mute the clear teaching of Scripture and the call to discipleship and call it compassion. Or they ignore the problem altogether for the sake of false unity and call it obedience to the Great Commission.

Abiding in Christ does not allow us to veer off in only one of these directions. Jesus intends for us to follow him down a path that only he knows. The Spirit is our guide, because Jesus sent him to us as a witness (vv. 26–27). As we follow the teaching of the apostles who walked and talked with Jesus, we can hear clearly the voice of Jesus calling us through the cacophony of the world.

Whatever direction the world tries to steer us—toward retreat, compromise, or assimilation—the Spirit points us to Jesus, the true north on our moral compass. Only when we abide in him will we resist the cares of the world and the snares of the flesh. You will hear some say that the world's opposition is a sign Christians must recalibrate. But Jesus told us to expect enmity from our enemies:

> If the world hates you, know that it has hated me before it hated you. If you were of the world, the world would love you as its own; but because you are not of the world, but I chose you out of the world, therefore the world hates you. Remember the word that I said to you: "A servant is not greater than his master." If they persecuted me, they will also persecute you. (vv. 18–20)

As a result, others view hatred from the world as confirmation that we're headed in the right direction. They scorn Christians who care too much about the love of the world. But the same Jesus indicated that when we abide in him, the world would know God's love by seeing our love for one another.

> I do not ask for these only, but also for those who will believe in me through their word, that they may all be one, just as you, Father, are in me, and I in you, that they also may be in us, so that the world may believe that you have sent me. The glory that you have given me I have given to them, that they may be one even as we are one, I in them and you in me, that they may become perfectly one, so that the world may know that you sent me and loved them even as you loved me. Father, I desire that they also, whom you have given me, may be with me

where I am, to see my glory that you have given me because you loved me before the foundation of the world. O righteous Father, even though the world does not know you, I know you, and these know that you have sent me. I made known to them your name, and I will continue to make it known, that the love with which you have loved me may be in them, and I in them. (John 17:20–26)

So the kind of biblical fullness that takes after Jesus expects opposition from the world and seeks unity among believers for the sake of the world. Isn't that fullness precisely what we see in the early church? Find hope in their faithful example! The apostles commissioned by Jesus courageously preached the crucified and resurrected Christ before hostile crowds. They demonstrated compassion in healing lame beggars and sharing their possessions and belongings with believers. They did their part to fulfill the Great Commission by bearing the good news about Jesus from Jerusalem to Samaria to Rome and beyond. These first Christians demonstrated what it means to abide in Christ. Though gifted in different ways, they showed the world a church where sinners could find joy, forgiveness, unity, and strength.

Muck of the World

Do not lose heart, because eventually the beauty of the gospel will shine through the muck of the world. God faithfully confounds any pursuit that does not result in abundant life. Our world cannot deny its Creator and enjoy its fruits forever. Today we have better technology, better health, and better knowledge of science than our ancestors did. But we're not measurably happier. We pride ourselves in progressive values. But new weapons and media give us greater ability to air and act on our intolerance and judgment. Outrage fills our days, stoked by talk radio, cable news, Facebook feeds, and Twitter streams. We've devoted billions to studying the inner workings of the brain and concluded that we're slaves to our impulses and circumstances.

Against such opposition, it's often easier for Christians to weep over the world than to pick up its pieces. But this is the world Jesus called us to love—not only in word or talk but in deed and truth (1 John 3:18). We must love as Jesus first loved us (1 John 4:19). He loved a world that rejected him, and so must we.

Consider the oft-cited example of William Wilberforce. For decades in the late 1700s and early 1800s he denounced the slave trade. It appears to us in hindsight like an obvious sin, but it was anything but obvious to the political and economic powers of his day. Wilberforce battled against various kinds of opposition, whether in the form of personal detractors or racism and systemic economic injustices. But you'll miss the significance of his ministry unless you understand how much his neighbors hated him for loving them. They called the evil of slavery good, but he loved them enough to endure their scorn in order to deliver them from this cruel bondage toward men and women made in God's image.

Like many other geniuses ahead of his time, Wilberforce

did not benefit from a world that initially understood his faith working through love as justice. So how did he overcome the world with love? He claimed citizenship in God's kingdom and looked forward to a day when the world would be as Jesus taught his disciples to pray: "on earth as it is in heaven" (Matt. 6:10b). When the situation looked bleak, Wilberforce abided in Jesus for strength to pursue the kind of justice on earth that anticipates the love that will ultimately prevail in Christ's return.

In one man we see a powerful example of biblical fullness. No one could fault Wilberforce for blind spots. You don't take on the banks and members of Parliament unless you've been inspired by the courage of Christ denouncing the religious and political authorities of his day. You don't look upon these suffering servants in compassion unless you've been saved from sin by the ultimate suffering servant, who was "pierced for our transgressions" and "crushed for our iniquities" (Isa. 53:5). And you don't persevere through countless setbacks unless you rest in Jesus's Great Commission promise: "I am with you always, to the end of the age" (Matt. 28:20).

Though Wilberforce triumphed, slavery persists in different forms today. Maybe nothing so brutally reveals the muck of our world as sex trafficking. So, inspired by the example of Wilberforce and ultimately governed by the commandment of Christ, how can believers cooperate to fight this evil in our day? Not everyone has the courage to raid a brothel in Bangkok and rescue the women. Not everyone has the compassion to nurse them to physical health and patiently help them trust in other people and God. Not everyone can coordinate an awareness campaign and mobilize the public to stem the demand for these shameful services. And if we with different gifts see only our own roles as necessary, our efforts will fail. If, however, we can appreciate how God has gifted others, together we can accomplish great good against all odds in a way that makes much of our King.

Do you believe it's possible? Or will you be blind to the need to work together and fail to see our differences as God-given opportunities? If you abide with Christ, long to obey his commandments, trust him to overcome the opposition of the world, and pursue unity among Christians with love, then ask God to end sex trafficking, and he might be so bold as to employ you in making it so.

I assume if you're reading this book you want to be used by God for his glory and the good of the world. So let me help you test whether your church could be so employed by God. Do you see unbelievers repenting of their sin and coming to new faith? Do you see believers growing to look more like Christ and less like the world even as they love their neighbors in the world? If you're walled off from the world, you can't love your neighbors and preach the gospel. If you're in the world and not confronting sin, then your neighbors can't repent and believe the good news about Jesus. And if you're in the world preaching the gospel but not calling new believers to costly discipleship, then you won't see them live by the Spirit and grow into Christ.

Be encouraged: I see many of these churches around the world. Maybe you even belong to one. I would not be surprised to see God raise up many new Wilberforces in our day. You might not see these gospel communities on the local news or read about them on your favorite blog. The counterrevolution of grace will not be televised. But if you're blessed to belong to such a body of believers, you know how they bring joy to your service and richness to your life. These *courageous, compassionate*, and *commissioned* churches stand like a city on a hill that cannot be hidden (Matt. 5:14). Don't you want to see Jesus answer your prayers and verify his teaching in your neighborhood? "Let your light shine before others, so that they may see your good works and give glory to your Father who is in heaven" (Matt. 5:16).

Don't wait for other Christians to lead the way. Don't judge yourself by their standard. Keep your eyes fixed on Jesus, and he will never fail you: "In the world you will have tribulation. But take heart; I have overcome the world" (John 16:33). Trust in the Spirit to guide you into all truth (v. 13) by anchoring you in God's Word. Here you'll find the *courage* to face the day. Here you'll be moved by *compassion* to return your enemy's hate with love. Here you'll be *commissioned* to take the gospel to all nations. Read, pray, and meditate on these words alone and in the company of those who share in your struggle to obey everything Jesus commanded. Abide in Christ and his love will carry you through many trials in the world and deliver you home as a good and faithful servant.

The best news of all is that no less than Jesus himself prays to our heavenly Father that such love would abide in and between us. God will not fail to hear and answer this prayer when we offer it in Jesus's name.

> I do not ask for these only, but also for those who will believe in me through their word, that they may all be one, just as you, Father, are in me, and I in you, that they also may be in us, so that the world may believe that you have sent me. (John 17:20–21)

Jesus secures our faith in the promise that a divided church that often garbles his witness to the world can testify with one voice to the only hope in any age.

Notes

1. Richard Lints, *The Fabric of Theology: A Prolegomena to Evangelical Theology* (Grand Rapids, MI: Eerdmans, 1993), 172.
2. Ibid.
3. Mark Noll, "Jonathan Edwards and Nineteenth-Century Theology," in *Jonathan Edwards and the American Experience*, ed. Nathan O. Hatch and Harry S. Stout (New York: Oxford University Press, 1989).
4. The quote about originality is from Lints, *Fabric of Theology*, 172n60. Old Princeton began with its first teacher, Archibald Alexander, a convert of the revivals, who was closest to Edwards in his integrative emphasis on sound theology and deep piety. (See his *Thoughts on Religious Experience*.) Perhaps understandably, Charles Hodge was cooler to revivalism in light of its excesses under Charles Finney and, after Hodge, Warfield gave the subject of religious experience very little focus.
5. Lints, *Fabric of Theology*, 261–62.
6. See Noll, "Jonathan Edwards and Nineteenth-Century Theology," 280–87.
7. Noll discusses two others who largely combined the emphases on cultural engagement, solid orthodoxy, and religious experience: the American theologian Henry B. Smith and Thomas Chalmers of the Free Church of Scotland. Ibid., 271–75.
8. Lausanne Movement, "The Lausanne Covenant," accessed June 19, 2014, http://www.lausanne.org/en/documents/lausanne-covenant.html.

9. http://www.ccel.org/ccel/richardson/fathers.x.i.ii.html.

10. C. S. Lewis, *Surprised by Joy: The Shape of My Early Life* (San Diego, CA: Harcourt, 1955), 107.

11. The Gospel Coalition, "Theological Vision of Ministry," accessed June 19, 2014, http://thegospelcoalition.org/about/foundation -documents.

12. I recommend Taylor Branch, *Parting the Waters: America in the King Years 1954–63* (New York: Simon & Schuster, 1989).

General Index

"50 Shades of Grace," 25
9/11 terrorist attacks, 98

abortion, 77
Adam, 43–44
African-Americans, 48, 74
alarmism, 65
Alexander, Archibald, 119n4
apostles, the, 22, 113
authority, 107–8

Baptists, 85
Bible, the, 84–85; reliability of, 78
biblical fullness, 109–13, 115
blind spots, 35, 37, 70, 90, 92; hope
     as a blind spot, 66; revealing of,
     22–23; suffering from, 111
Bush, George W., 75

capitalism, inequity of, 48
charity, 78
Chesterton, G. K., 54–55
Christian fellowship, 20
Christianity, 16–17, 19, 41, 72, 92,
     97; as an à la carte faith, 90; at-
     traction to, 73; and culture, 93;
     distinctive doctrines of, 31
Christians, 15, 16, 17, 44–45, 53, 83,
     93, 111, 113, 114, 117; as am-
bassadors of the good news and
peace, 27–28; attitude of toward
suffering, 28; Christian leaders,
19; commissioned Christians,
84, 85–86, 88, 89–90, 100, 108;
conservative Christians, 74;
criticism of, 72; and cynicism,
66; Egyptian Christians, 98; gifting of by God, 26, 107–8; iden-
tification as, 25–26; judgmental
Christians, 57; "know-it-all
Christians," 26; love of among
Christians, 26, 29; "only-issue
Christians," 33–34; and political
movements, 77; preoccupa-
tion of with the battle between
fundamentalists and modernists,
31; Roman perception of, 75–76;
skepticism of, 21, 31; temptation of, 29; unifying of, 95
church, the, of Jesus, 39, 95; commissioned churches, 86–87, 92;
making the church a welcoming
place, 70; mission statements of,
100; of the New Testament, 104;
unity of despite the diversity
of spiritual gifts of its members,
104–9
civil rights movement, 74, 77

121

Scripture Index

Also Available from **Crossway** and The Gospel Coalition